MW01063211

MAN OF GOD

MAN OF
GOD

Lessons to Young Men About
Life, Sex, Friendship, Vocation,
& Loving with the Heart of Christ

Terrence P. Ehrman, C.S.C.

Catholic
Answers
Press

Man of God

© 2017 Terrence P. Ehrman, C.S.C.

Published by Catholic Answers, Inc.
2020 Gillespie Way
El Cajon, California 92020
1-888-291-8000 orders
619-387-0042 fax

catholic.com

Printed in the United States of America
Interior design by Claudine Mansour Design

978-1-68357-027-1
978-1-68357-028-8 Kindle
978-1-68357-029-5 ePub

CONTENTS

ACKNOWLEDGEMENTS

Thanks be to God, the Most Adorable Trinity, in whose providence this work was completed. I thank my parents, Jim and Mary Ann Ehrman, whose love for their five children within a Catholic marriage—now spanning fifty-four years— was the ground in which the seed for this book was planted. Friendships spanning nearly two decades with married couples and their families inspired, transformed, and taught me about love and faith. I thank, in particular, Tammye and Bob Raster, Mary and Mitch Walorski, and Roger and Chrissy Klauer. I also thank the many consecrated religious of the Dominican Sisters of St. Cecilia, Religious Sisters of Mercy of Alma, and Franciscan Sisters of the Eucharist whom I have known and who have supported me with friendship and prayer and have been eschatological signs of hope of life in the fullness of the kingdom.

This work has gone through several stages of development. I thank Sr. M. Timothy Prokes, F.S.E., for her comments on the original version of this manuscript. This book in its present form would not have been possible, however, without the labors of Eileen Mallon Evans, who read and edited the work, making insightful and wise suggestions as to content and style. Finally, I thank Todd Aglialoro at Catholic Answers Press for his careful eye, cogent editing, motivation, and his patience.

INTRODUCTION

I first met Joseph seven years ago when, as a junior in college, he enrolled in my fall semester theology course, Human Sexuality and the Sacrament of Marriage. Over the next year and a half until he graduated, Joseph would periodically stop by my office or my room in the residence hall to talk about faith and struggles he, like many of his peers, had concerning chastity and purity—especially pornography and its associated effects.

After graduation, Joseph moved back to the Midwest and started a job in Chicago with a consulting firm. During that first year out of college, he would e-mail to keep in touch and also to keep tabs on his sister, who was a year behind him and also taking my class. Joseph returned to campus for his sister's graduation the next year, and it was then that he asked me if I would provide regular long-distance spiritual direction to help him with his continuing struggles with chastity. I agreed, and we began an e-mail correspondence.

Not long ago I was passing through Chicago and met up with Joseph. During a conversation about his maturation over the course of the year, he reflected that all young men, particularly college students and recent graduates, would benefit from the kind of exchange we had been having. His comment gave me an idea: what if I published an edited version of my e-mail responses to him? Wouldn't this be a form of spiritual direction for others? He agreed. So, what follows is my half of the correspondence with him. I've edited it slightly to make it apparent to what concerns and circumstances I was responding and to keep some names and places anonymous.

I hope that you find these e-mails helpful. Your own history and situations may differ from Joseph's, but I think the truth contained in these letters is universally applicable to men of today—whether younger or older—from whatever background. May the Holy Spirit, the ultimate spiritual director, free you from the darkness of lust and form you in a life of true, chaste manhood and freedom in Christ.

God bless,

Fr. Terry Ehrman

MAN OF GOD

To: **Joseph**

Date: **June 23—Feast of the Sacred Heart**

Re: **HEART SPEAKS TO HEART**

Dear Joseph,

May the peace and strength of the Holy Spirit be with you on this feast of the Sacred Heart of Jesus. I read your e-mail late last night, and I am glad you enjoyed your week-long business meeting in Seattle, your first time in the state of Washington. The natural setting is quite different from Chicago for sure. Though both are on water, the dominance of Mt. Rainier creates a whole different feel. You enjoyed Puget Sound and Pike Place Market, took in a Mariners game, and even made it to Mass last Sunday for Corpus Christi at the cathedral of St. James. You were pleasantly surprised by the plaque in the vestibule that described St. Frances Xavier Cabrini's presence in Seattle ministering to the Italian immigrants, just as she did in Chicago. The view of Mt. Rainier from your hotel room sounds breathtaking!

Though the natural beauty and conference excursions

were refreshing, the work was intense, and you found yourself alone at night in your hotel room, tired and feeling isolated. You found company in the manner you have been accustomed to since graduating from college two years ago: internet pornography. In order not to have your activity traced through room charges for downloading porn to the television and because you had the company laptop, you resorted to your smartphone. Each night repeated the pattern of pornography and masturbation. The banter in the hotel bar among male colleagues about the attractive women at the conference only fueled your sexual desires. I am glad you said you were heading to confession this weekend now that you are back home.

I've been pondering your use of the words "finding yourself" seeking out porn websites and "falling into" sin. Is it really so passive? You are the one who *chooses* and *decides* to swipe your finger across the screen and plunge yourself into the pornographic waters. Joseph, what is the condition of your heart when you touch your finger to that familiar screen? What is your heart yearning for, and are the sought-after images the answer? Do they satisfy your heart? Or do they only anesthetize the deep desire? Isn't your heart yearning instead for real human communion where you encounter another person heart to heart?

These internet images of naked bodies are untouchable and the hearts of the actual women hidden and inaccessible. The pornographic venture is an inherent contradiction. It cannot satisfy. The naked woman on the screen only exists as a servant to your sexual pleasure. You cannot speak to her, and she cannot speak to you. You cannot ask her the condition of her heart.

I think your pangs of conscience indicate that you know, deep within, that you want to be someone different. You know that being a man of the world, though comfortable, is ultimately empty. Your heart tells you that you are made for more. You are made to be a man of God.

When the great John Henry Newman became a cardinal, he chose the motto *cor ad cor loquitur*—heart speaks to heart. "I" meet "you." Are you prepared to meet another person heart to heart? I often wonder what it would be like to greet a friend, or colleague, or the neighbor next door, and ask, "How is your heart?" Unlike perfunctory questions like, "How are you?" or "How are you doing?" that question truly seeks an answer. "How is your heart?" intensifies the level of relationship and raises the interaction to a fuller human level. One heart seeks to engage another, asking for confidence and trust.

Open your heart to me. What brings it joy? Of what does it need to be healed or forgiven? When asked in love, the question takes two hearts and draws them together.

"How is your heart?" is a question about the core of our humanity. Who are you? Who do you long to be? What is your relationship with sin and grace? It's also ultimately a question about your relationship with God. What is the relationship of your heart to those in your family, in your community of friends, and to those with whom you work or whom you serve? What is the relationship of your heart to the Sacred Heart of Jesus?

On this feast of the Sacred Heart of Jesus, I offer Christ

as the fulfillment of the longing of every human heart. The Sacred Heart is a portal to the love of the Trinity. The Sacred Heart reveals God's love for us in Jesus Christ, who was sent by the Father to draw all humankind, every person from every time and place and background—you and me and the women in the pornographic videos you watch—every human heart to the Father through himself in the Holy Spirit. He encounters each person heart to heart. He invites us to share in the communion of divine love that he shares with the Father and Holy Spirit.

So, how do you meet the heart of another in this trinitarian love?

First, let me say that sexual attraction and desires are good and natural to us. They are a gift from God, who made us male and female. He gave us these desires to be ordered to the good, governed by the virtues, and guided by the Holy Spirit's vivifying power. But lust corrupts sexual desire, ordering it toward selfishness. It leads not to encountering another person but to possessing her, imprisoning her in the smallness of your imagination.

Instead of living with an impoverished and impure heart that looks upon the body of a woman with selfish desire, dwell in your heart with Christ and see with his eyes the fullness of the *person* who stands before you. Read those passages from Sacred Scripture in which our Lord encounters women: Peter's mother-in-law (Luke 4); the grieving widow of Nain (Luke 7); the sinful woman who wept on his feet (Luke 7); Mary Magdalene and the other women who followed him (Luke 8); the woman with the hemorrhage and the daughter of Jairus (Luke 8); the crippled woman (Luke 13); and the widow with the two coins (Luke 21). John's Gospel provides two more developed accounts of meetings with women: the Samaritan at the well (John 4) and the woman caught in adultery (John 8).

Read these passages and meditate on how Jesus encountered these women. How did he look at them? What did they see as their eyes met his? How did his heart speak to their hearts? How did he touch them? What did he have to give them? What was his desire? Imagine Jesus placing his hands on their faces and looking into their eyes. Those women knew they were loved for who they were and not for what they could do for him.

Note, too, the range of women encountered: the young, the elderly, the sick, the mourning, the contrite. Meditate on the expanse of Jesus' love in comparison to the narrow focus of lust's gaze, and practice expanding your own range of vision. Be attentive to whom you desire to look at. When you open up your web browser to check the news, where do your eyes go? To the ubiquitous sensual advertisements? Discipline your heart to gaze from your heart upon the starving woman, the elderly refugee, the homeless woman without any teeth, and the woman who is frumpy or lonely. See them with the eyes of Christ.

When you are at work, at the grocery store, at Mass, whom do you seek to see? Do you focus only on those who are sexually attractive? Do you scope the aisles or the pews for only the pretty women? Make his heart your heart. At the parish coffee and doughnuts social after Mass, purposely look at and even introduce yourself to the person to whom you are not physically attracted. Look upon the people and be attentive not just to the "beautiful" women, but to the expanse of ages and shapes and faces. Expand your heart in love. Then, even when you look at young and attractive women, your heart will have been formed to look at them with love and not lust.

The greater expanse of Jesus' vision helps form us to be men of love and to situate our sexual desires and attractions within the fullness of our personhood.

In contrast, pornography stagnates the heart and its growth. Like any evil, pornography cannot create; it only perverts and corrupts the true and the real into a false imitation. In viewing pornography, you do not create but only pervert the goodness of God's Creation as you objectify the human person and "use" her for your selfish pleasure.

We are not to "use" people. St. Augustine adroitly compared "use" and "enjoy." We are to *enjoy* God's presence and, in him, to enjoy the presence and friendship of people, but we are to *use* things. We sin in doing the reverse—using God and people and enjoying things. Through pornography and lust, you use people. People become mere things of our lust and imagination. You do not encounter a person but a phantasm to be manipulated and dominated. You isolate yourself from God's world and immerse yourself in "your" world, a stasis in which there is no growth, no life, and only a timeless shadowy image to be forced to follow your will. Lust and the absence of personhood, the absence of mutual self-gift that exists between a man and woman in love, perpetuates the sin of Adam who "lords" himself over his beloved's desire for him (Gen. 3:16).

JOSEPH, IN ORDER to overcome lust, you must dwell in the heart. You must encounter Love himself. Love will make you a person, an authentic person who lives in freedom. Love calls us to and embeds us in relationships with other persons. The most important relationship, of course, is with the Father through Christ in the Holy Spirit, and that relationship will correctly order all of our other relationships. Our relationship with God is our *prayer*.

How is your prayer? Certainly, we are to set aside definite times throughout the day for prayer, but more so, we are, as St. Paul exhorts the Thessalonians, to pray without ceasing. Every moment of our lives is an opportunity to be in union with God. He is always aware of us; we are just not always aware of him. Do we tremble with awe and delight before the tremendous mystery that is the Trinity? Is your prayer a lover's gaze upon our Beloved? So often our prayer is rushed and distracted, as if we would rather be with someone else. St. Mechtilde described prayer in this way: "Prayer is naught else but a yearning of the heart. It draws the great God down into the tiny heart. It drives the hungry soul up into the plenitude of God. It brings together these two lovers, God and the soul, in a wondrous place where they speak of love." Is that your prayer?

I often wonder how Jesus prayed. "Rising early before the dawn, he left that place . . . and went out to pray" (Mark 1:35). Jesus went out into the hillsides around the Sea of Galilee to be alone—to be alone with his Father. In the silence, solitude, and stillness he prayed. What was his prayer like? What would it be like to witness the Son praying to the Father in the Holy Spirit? His prayer was a deep communion, an intense love and oneness. From that deep place of prayer, Jesus preached and healed and performed great works and ultimately gave himself up to death on a cross. How can you pray like that?

In the union of the Holy Spirit, Jesus encounters his Father in solitude and silence. What depth of love, what intensity of union, what trust and obedience! The Father! He is the dynamic, primal source of all that is—the unoriginate source of the Trinity and of all Creation. He is the fountain fullness of life and love and goodness and truth and beauty. Jesus was sent by the Father to show us the way to the Father: "I am the way, the truth, and the life" (John 14:6). The Holy Spirit, that Spirit of purity and life, has been poured into your heart to make of you a new creation, to sanctify you, and to give you eternal life.

Is your prayer merely an obedience, a task to be completed? Or is it vital? Is your *faith* vital? Thomas Merton, the Trappist priest and monk, said, "There is only one source of truth, but . . . it is not sufficient to know the source is there—we must go and drink from it." Do you drink deep from the fountain of the Father?

Our faith is not the mere recitation of prayers or profession of dogmas and formulas. The formulas are attempts to understand the tremendous mystery of God and our encounter of the divine Trinity. Merton continues, "What too often has been overlooked, in consequence, is that Catholicism is the taste and experience of eternal life." That is not a flat or stale faith. Being a Catholic is about drinking deep of the life-giving waters that originate in the Father and create and save us. At that source, all is holy. No darkness, no lust, no selfishness. Do you strive to dwell in your heart so that every thought, every intention, every word, and every action flows from your union with that fountain?

So, how do you dwell at this wellspring of life? One way is to pray with attention, to practice contemplative prayer. This kind of prayer is the prayer of Mary who sits at the feet of Jesus while her sister Martha labors in the kitchen. It is a prayer of the heart enjoying the divine presence. A Russian mystic instructed others when they prayed "to descend with the mind into the heart, and there to stand before the face of the Lord, ever-present, all-seeing within you." Contemplative prayer is particularly useful in countering lust, for this discipline of prayer requires the integration of the body and spirit.

The conditions for contemplative prayer are silence and stillness and solitude. Created in the image of God, our hearts are made for prayer—to go up into the hills before dawn and unite ourselves with him. Unfortunately, as you know, our culture is *not* made for prayer. We are bombarded with noise, images, and motion—commotion—such that our hearts find no rest. Urban life in particular blares at us incessantly. We can fear to enter the silence of our heart. We fear being alone by ourselves in a room full of silence. Wasn't this the case in your Seattle hotel room?

The first step of contemplative prayer is to find a place of stillness and silence and solitude at a time of the day when you are most alert so that you can give your best to God.

Thus, don't pray on a full stomach—your mind is too cloud-
ed. Prayer and fasting go together; the mind is also clear and
alert just after exercise. Next, attend to your breath. The spiritual masters note the relationship of our breath to our spirits.
The words for breath and spirit, in both Hebrew (*ruah*) and
Greek (*pneuma*), are the same. Attentive to each breath, you
grow attentive to God, whose breath is the source of life itself.
Take slow, deep breaths, and exhale gently, soft like a baby's
breath. Try to take about four to five breaths a minute.

Body posture is also important. For example, sit upright on
a chair. Attentive to each breath, speak a word or phrase that
helps attend to God—perhaps the word "God," or "Father,
Son, and Holy Spirit"; or in the ancient tradition of the Eastern monks, the Jesus Prayer from Luke's Gospel: "Jesus Christ,
Son of the living God, have mercy on me, a sinner" (18:13).
Focus yourself in your heart. With each inhalation, imagine
Jesus Christ abiding in your heart and his Spirit permeating
your body, reaching every part, even those dark, unconscious
parts, transforming them and filling them with light. With
each exhalation expel anything dark and unholy. Coordi-
nate those words with your breath, and repeat them over and
over. That word or phrase helps root us in the onslaught of
thoughts that break loose once our mind is quieted, just as a
river drops its load of sediment when it runs into a lake—so,
too, your heart when you enter into silence. A whirlwind of
thoughts swirl about. Our attention on God should be as singular as our attention on escape if someone yelled "Fire!" in
a crowded room.

This focused attention brings a new conception of life, of

love, of people, of God. A new way of being that has no place or even desire for lust's denigration of humanity. In the stillness and silence and solitude, you descend into your heart and encounter God. Prayer is about being aware of God at all times. There was never a time in which Jesus was not aware of the Father. Every thought, word, action, and touch of Jesus was a result of his deep intimacy with the Father. How do you become a man of prayer so that every word, action, thought, and decision emerges from a deep place of prayer and oneness with God? You may pray contemplatively for just five or ten minutes each day, but you can attend to God always. Every moment of your life is an opportunity for prayer: standing in line at the grocery store, stuck in traffic on the highway, washing the dishes, or confined to a mind-numbing business meeting. In each of those moments, you can pray from your heart. Why would you choose to sin, when you dwell in that Blessed Realm of God?

In prayer, we collect ourselves. Usually, we are scattered and spread out all over the place. But in prayer, you stand here in this place; you are aware of yourself and make decisions from a vantage point of freedom and love. Your heart deepens and expands, and you engage another in the vastness of God's love, that realm in which you live in prayer. In prayer, you enter into your heart and encounter God. You become collected and gathered. Karl Rahner, a twentieth-century Jesuit theologian, reflected that the man of the heart is the one "whose whole activity is an exhaustive expression of his innermost center and his innermost vital decision, and who therefore remains 'collected' in this innermost center without being dispersed in anything alien to this decision." Lust, pornography, and self-pleasure are all alien to the pure, "collected" man.

The extent to which you are able to engage God with intense, single-minded intimacy in prayer is a measure of how well you are able to engage with people. When you meet others, when you talk to others, do you look them in the eye? Does your heart meet theirs? How do you grow in maturity such that your heart can meet the heart of another? You can be scattered all over the place—you look at your shoes or off to the side; you speak from a place of fear rather than a place of love in which you can reveal yourself to another. The more you dwell in your heart, the more you will see the emptiness and falsehood of lust as something that does not measure up to the dignity of your true desires and of your personhood.

Joseph, be a man with a sacred heart. Be a "collected" man. Be a man of God. As we pray in the conclusion of litany of the Sacred Heart, make your heart *according to his heart*. Pray without ceasing and draw close to the Father through Christ in the Holy Spirit. *Cor ad cor loquitur.*

Be assured of my prayer for you, particularly at the holy sacrifice of the Mass, where we are most intimately united in the Mystical Body of Christ.

In the Sacred Heart of Jesus,

Fr. Terry

PS:

—Pray contemplatively each day by entering into your heart, where God makes his home in you.

—Learn to look at others, especially women, from a place of love and truth.

—Be a man of God!

2

To: **Joseph**

Date: **July 16—Our Lady of Mt. Carmel**

Re: PROTECTING YOUR GARDEN

Dear Joseph,

May the purity and truth of the Holy Spirit be with your spirit to help you in your struggles.

Joseph, you wrote of bodily passions and desires that are inflamed by an untethered imagination. You've struggled with internet pornography and masturbation as you seek comfort for your tiredness and stress after long hours of work. Sexual fantasies with the bodies of unknown and unnamed women provide a release from the demands of real life. You wrote about the rush of pleasure you feel as you abandon yourself to the bodies on the screen before you. At work, you eagerly await going home to open the internet door to what you call the "garden of delight." Once you start viewing images and videos, you don't want to stop. Only your own exhaustion or the necessity of getting some sleep to be functional at work the next day brings the pleasure reluctantly to a hiatus until the next night.

Your immersion into pornography is not only from tiredness and stress, you admitted, but also from lingering sexual imaginings about an attractive new woman in the office. Because of the training schedule, you haven't really met Lisa; you've only seen her a couple of times. But those brief sightings have unsettled your heart with lust. Joseph, remember all that I wrote last month about prayer and encountering another heart to heart. Now, I want to develop how being a man of God requires discipline to protect yourself and others from lust.

First, I want to take up your image of the "garden of delight," which is actually a reference to the Garden of Eden. (In the Sumerian language, the word *Eden* designates a fertile plain, and a Hebrew cognate for it means "delight.") Pornographers draw upon the naked bodies of Adam and Eve in this garden of delight as they try to entice viewers to enter into a garden whose sole purpose is abandonment to sexual pleasure. They create their own mythic universe, a revised story about human origins in which man and woman are created just for the sake of sexual pleasure with one another. But this pornographic Eden is not God's garden but the serpent's. (When the story of Adam and Eve was written in the tenth century B.C., the fertility cults of the neighboring peoples tempted the people of Israel to idolatry through participation in their sexual rites. The symbol of these cults was a serpent!)

I want to show you the true Garden of Eden. On this Marian feast of Our Lady of Mt. Carmel, I find myself at a Mary Garden. Over the centuries, Christians associated various flowers with different events and virtues of the life of the Blessed Virgin Mary and planted gardens with these flowers around a statue of Our Lady. This morning, soft yellow sunshine alights upon this company of flowers. Morning glory's purple and blue trumpet-like corollas proclaim hymns of praise from graded heights upon the wooden trellis that runs along the length of the garden's back wall. Alyssum's incense of sweet fragrance arises from snowball clusters of white flowers. Mary's purity reveals itself in lavender's sweet scent while yellow marigolds reflect her golden glory. Yellow flag irises stand humbly obedient around Our Lady's statue; these yellow sentinels emerge from moist soil on the small circular island central to the garden. The placid ring of water surrounding the island displays yellow and white water lilies. Smooth-barked crepe myrtles adorned in eruptions of white and red sprays, and the redbuds and dogwoods, whose blossoms filled the spring with wonder, shepherd their smaller charges.

This walled garden refreshes the spirit with its quiet solitude and stillness. The soul here encounters an Eden-like purity. The heart encounters Mary's Immaculate Heart. Our Lady is the New Eve who is Virgin, Mother, and Bride. "She is a garden enclosed, my sister, my promised bride, a garden enclosed, a sealed fountain" (Song of Sol. 4:12). This Mary Garden, this New Eden, also reflects the beauty of Mt. Carmel in the Holy Land, whose natural splendor bespeaks the beauty of God: "Let the wilderness and the dry lands exult, let the wasteland rejoice and bloom, let it bring forth flowers like the jonquil, let it rejoice and sing for joy. The glory of

Lebanon is bestowed on it, the splendor of Carmel and Sharon; they shall see the glory of the Lord, the splendor of our God" (Isa. 35:2).

Joseph, *our souls* are to be enclosed gardens where God walks in the cool of the day, a blessed realm of beauty both virginal and fecund: virginal in its purity and faithful singularity of love and adoration of the Trinity, and fecund in its fruit of virtue, nobility of words, and charitable acts. The virginal heart is pure and enclosed, deliberately bounded to protect the sacred dignity of our being. The virginal heart is purposeful, its every act and thought intentional. The virginal heart assiduously tends the garden, removing weeds without delay, and it tirelessly inspects the integrity of the gate and walls. The virginal heart is vigilant and patiently expectant. The virginal heart relies on the Lord more than a watchman on the coming of the dawn. The virginal heart takes its fill of the fruits of Wisdom: "They who eat me will hunger for more, they who drink me will thirst for more" (Sir. 24:21). The virginal heart burns with love to be in the presence of Christ at the banquet table. The virginal heart "follows the Lamb wherever he goes" (Rev. 14:4) and comes to share in the Master's joy.

Sadly, many souls have neglected their gardens. The rusted gates and crumbling walls all too easily allow entrance to those who do not belong. Your past descriptions of college life and of the current nighttime social life among your workplace peers reveal those who invite strangers into their gardens. Such is the situation with men and women seeking casual hookup sexual encounters—those seeking to breach others' gardens or to lure others into theirs. Other breaches are simply voyeuristic, with so many souls slack at the watch, unaware of the precious dignity of their being.

Our world races to expose what should be hidden, to give oneself away to another who has not the capacity or the right to receive the giver. Instead be like Daniel, who preserved the integrity, purity, and virtue of Susanna, a married woman falsely accused by two elders of the community appointed as judges. These nameless elders lusted after Susanna, a beautiful and faithful daughter of Israel: "Making no effort to turn their eyes to heaven . . . they contrived to see her every day" (Dan. 13:9, 12) so that they could feast on her beauty. Seeking refreshment one day from the heat, Susanna entered her enclosed garden to bathe, and once the door was closed, the elders, who had surreptitiously entered the garden, swept upon her as vultures wanting her flesh. Preferring to remain innocent in the eyes of God rather than sin, Susanna cried out for help. The elders falsely accused her, saying that they had discovered Susanna with a young lover who had escaped their grasp. Vindictively, the elders condemned Susanna to death by stoning. God answered Susanna's prayer for justice by sending the young Daniel to reveal the falsehood and malice of the elders and to vindicate Susanna's innocence.

Joseph, who will you be? Daniel or the salacious elders? A man of honor and guardian of purity or a self-indulgent breacher of garden walls? Will you govern and guide your passions with self-mastery, or will you be a slave to desires and temptations? The elders abandoned themselves—their reason—to sensory delight. Their lust blinded their minds, and their gluttony dulled their senses. They hunted Susanna like predators seeking a meal, unconcerned with her person and will; they stole into her garden to feast on her body and defile her purity.

Venery is the art of hunting, but it also has a secondary meaning of pursuit of sexual indulgence. The venery of those elders of ancient times is the same as feasting upon the bodies of women today, whether on the internet or in person. Pornography exposes that which should remain hidden; it breaches the wall of the enclosed garden and spies lecherously upon another. The lustful heart gazes upon women at parties, at the store, at church, at work, forcing its way into the reserved garden.

BE WARY, JOSEPH, of the temptation to idolize your own body, which leads to the desire for sexual self-gratification. With the onset of puberty, young men often develop a fascination with their own bodies and the powerful pleasure they can generate for themselves. The doodling of adolescent boys, the bathroom graffiti, the lascivious conversations and imaginations of college men focused on their own bodies, and the stereotypical lecherous old man are modern-day manifestations of an ancient and perhaps universal worship of the male procreative organ. The prophets admonished the people of Israel who had turned to the practices of their Canaanite neighbors by erecting phallic idols or engaging in ritual prostitution. Moses commanded the people of Israel to "smash their pillars, cut down their sacred poles" (Deut. 12:3). Like

Moses, be a man of God and smash the idolatrous pillars of lust that you have constructed in your heart. Protect the boundaries of your soul, and make it a sanctuary where you can worship God in spirit and in truth. *Blessed are the clean of heart for they shall see God.* The virtue of chastity brings a freedom for others and from self-absorption.

Self-fascination can lead to a self-indulgent life in which men are absorbed with their bodies and enslaved to the desire for orgasm. They constantly seek to satisfy themselves; instead of loving women for who they are, they want to be served and be satisfied by women. Instead of becoming a mature man, a man of God, they remain sexual adolescents whose interactions with women remain at the level of bodily satisfaction. They miss the depth and breadth of mature personhood; they miss a life of freedom in which passions and desires are directed in accord with the truth.

For some, sinful patterns of behavior become so habitual that they dominate the rest of that man's life. I know eighty-year-old men whose struggle with pornography and masturbation has remained unbroken since puberty. Many never reveal their sin, except perhaps in the confessional. Such a hiddenness, such an inability to reveal one's vulnerability, weakness, and sin only perpetuates an already selfish life. Solomon's wisdom teaches us that "he who conceals his faults will not prosper, he who confesses and renounces them will find mercy" (Prov. 28:13). Yes, we are to confess our sins in the sacrament of reconciliation, yet how do we grow in love and communion with the rest of the Body of Christ?

THE EARLY YEARS of developing sexual identity, character, and habits of being are critical. What type of garden will you create? How will you protect it? How will you be a servant of God and not a servant of pagan fertility gods? How will you live as a disciple of Christ as a male sexual being?

The word *disciple* comes from the Latin word "to learn." Thus, a disciple is a student, one who is learning to follow Christ. In the parable of the sower, the sowed seed fell in various environments: a paved path, among rocks, among thorns, and on good soil. The seed or plant is destroyed in the first three environments and only flourishes in the good soil. Joseph, you must till the ground of your garden, remove the rocks and weeds, and make a good soil for the Word of God to fall in and germinate. Discipline yourself. Discipline is the act of a disciple.

Discipline forms your character so that your actions are no longer haphazard, but directed. You begin to choose the good with quickness, ease, and joy. You become a man of God who is collected of mind, body, and spirit; a man of God who is whole and integrated. In contrast, the undisciplined man is divided and unsteady. Lust and obsession with self-pleasure are the fruits of his inner disruption.

Learning how to live as a disciplined man is more than mere obedience to a litany of cans and cannots. Sexual morality should not begin with asking, "What am I allowed or not allowed to do?" but rather, as Pope St. John Paul II asked, "How do I live a life of sexual love that is in accord with my dignity as a person created in the image and likeness of God?" You become holy not by a prudish avoidance of your sexual character but by a Spirit-permeated bodily life that delights in your body as a gift of God.

Many young men wonder how they could leave behind a life of sexual self-indulgence or why they would even want to. Many don't even think that indulging in pornography is wrong. *How can sex and pleasure be harmful? It's natural, and it feels good.*

As I wrote to you last month, sexuality and sexual desires are good. God has created us as sexual beings: male and female (Gen. 1:27). Sexuality is part of our human nature. As men and women, however, we are *persons* who are ordered toward one another in relationship. Our sexual desires, specifically, are ordered toward a *conjugal* relationship: marriage with one person of the other sex. Through pornography, though, the lustful heart seeks sexual pleasure for itself, ordered to no relationship, disconnected from its purposes. Lust dehumanizes. It reduces the fullness of a person to sexual parts and desires.

A disciplined man of God first respects the integrity of his own nature, but he must also be a man of justice who cares for the community. The participant in pornography who imagines that all the models and actresses are freely giving themselves for the pleasure of others blinds himself to the machinations of the industrial degradation of women, the evil manipulation of vulnerable girls and women, sex slavery, and the trampled dignity of women whose hearts have chosen a falsehood. Pornography is a favorite tool of the devil because it allows him to use a good—human sexuality—to snare willing and susceptible victims in a distortion and perversion of the truth.

THE FREEDOM TO act is rooted in knowing what is true and willing the good. Often we are ignorant about what is true, and we will a false good. We lack a unity of being; our passions are unruly, and our will is misdirected. Ask yourself, Joseph: is it *you* who chooses lust, or pornography, because it feels good and seems natural? Do *you* make the decision in freedom? Or do you feel like the decision is being made for you? Without discipline we can feel like slaves to our passions, servants rather than masters of our will.

Strive to regain your interior unity, to be a disciplined man. One important tool of the disciplined man is *fasting*. Fasting restores the unity of our being. It brings together body and spirit, with the soul asserting itself above mere physical instincts. In fasting, you make a deliberate decision of the will. It is *you* who chooses to fast and not your stomach or an impulse. You are attentive, aware, and vigilant about who you are and what you do. Your actions become intentional; you tell your instincts that you are their master.

Fasting is pointless if it is done as a mere routine to fulfill an obligation, disconnected from an aversion to sin and reconversion to God. Sin is a turning away from God, and you must continually turn back to him with your whole being—spirit and body. Fasting is a penance that says, "I want

to offer my whole self as a pleasing sacrifice to the Lord."
You may fast not just from food, but from any kind of good
thing, such as turning on the car radio, watching TV, drinking
coffee, or looking at e-mails before you have prayed in the
morning. Your abstaining from these activities increases your
capacity for self-denial. You would prefer to do them, but you
will resist. The fruit of such fasting is self-control. You govern
yourself rather than being governed by your desires or these
activities.

This discipline can, then, help you govern your sensual
desires. Thus, unlike the lecherous elders who never turned
their eyes to heaven and away from Susanna, you will able
to practice custody of the eyes when you see a woman—at
the beach or gym, in a TV or magazine ad, or at work, as for
example, with Lisa—upon whose body your eyes and mind
would seek to linger in lust. "To you have I lifted up my eyes,
you who dwell in the heavens" (Ps. 123). Discipline yourself
to turn your head or close your eyes. Know your masculine
nature: men are susceptible to lust and pornography because
we are visually stimulated. Be aware of this vulnerability, and
take steps to guard your soul from unseemly images and from
known occasions of sin and temptation.

Discipline yourself to turn away from *thoughts* as well.
Thoughts can come to you unbidden, and you can also intentionally generate them. Memory and imagination are powerful because through them, you live in another time and
place. You relive the past in memory. You anticipate or create
the future with imagination. But these powers, too, must be
your servants. Practice turning your attention away even from

harmless idle memories and imaginings and you will also train your mind against thoughts that can lead to sin: against imaginings of lust or envy, against memories of being wronged. Keep training your mind in this way, and these thoughts will diminish and have no power over you.

A colleague of mine shared with me about his sabbatical year in the San Francisco Bay Area. He would enjoy nights on the rooftop deck of his apartment, looking at the bay, the city, and the stars. One night, he unintentionally discovered that the neighbors' bathroom window made of glass block was translucent enough to give a rough silhouette of the person in the shower, namely the attractive wife who lived there. My friend not only had to find the discipline to turn his eyes away, but also not to let his imagination create a more exact figure, or to anticipate future nighttime observations. In his memory he had to wrestle with not calling this experience to mind and visualizing again what he had seen. It required the exercise of his will to direct his thoughts and deny himself.

You can also learn to discipline your unruly body directly with your will. Once, St. Benedict was tempted by an evil spirit and recalled a woman he had seen, which started to arouse his emotions. Almost overcome by his thoughts, Benedict immediately stripped off his garments and hurled himself naked into a patch of thorns and stinging nettles. He rolled and tossed and turned until the pain and blood had extinguished the evil passion in his heart. Benedict told his disciples that "he never experienced another temptation of this kind."

I don't recommend this practice for you, Joseph! But it is

an indication of how seriously the saints considered sin and how it took them away from Jesus Christ, who "endured the cross . . . and opposition from sinners. In your struggle against sin you have not yet resisted to the point of shedding blood" (Heb. 12:2-4). What are you willing to do to forgo lustful memories and imaginings about Lisa or to avoid searching for pornographic websites on your phone? (Years ago, when porn was primarily available only at public places—so-called "adult" bookstores and movie theaters—men could avoid occasions of sin by simply avoiding those places. Now, because we carry occasions of sin around with us in the privacy of our own laptops and our phones, we need much greater degrees of self-discipline!)

You do not need to follow the severity of St. Benedict's one-time action. There is another way of fasting and denial that is more gradual, but it requires the same firmness of purpose and aversion to sin that he had. In the monasteries, when confronted with temptation, some monks would begin to read a chapter of Sacred Scripture. If the desire persisted, they would read another chapter. By drawing near to the living Word of God, they turned their minds and hearts there and away from the sensual thoughts. Christ is the ultimate answer to temptation. You may also find it useful to turn your thoughts to images of people who suffer: a starving boy in Africa with a distended belly, an elderly woman without her teeth, or families who have lost their homes to natural disaster or war. These images get your heart loving; love calls forth mercy and compassion, which can't coexist with lust. Thinking with love about other people turns your thoughts to Christ, for what you do to your brothers and sisters in need, you do to him.

PRAY. LEARN TO quiet your heart. Practice resisting. Offer yourself to God in obedience. Pray Psalm 16: "Those who choose other gods increase their sorrows. Never will I offer their offerings of blood. Never will I take their name upon my lips." Call upon the Holy Spirit whose fruit is self-control. Go deep into your soul, far away from false bodily impulses, and draw near to the living flame of Love. Let that fire gradually burn away the dross of lust and falsehood. The Spirit of Love purifies our desires and strengthens our will.

As you deny vice, practice virtue. Seek to become a man of God, a tender man of honor with a sacred heart. Modesty. Purity. Uprightness. Make these your companions in your relationships with all people and especially with women. Guard your virginity. Guard the virginity of others. Be Daniel, ever protecting the dignity and purity of your sister Susannas. (The story of Susanna, without her hero, continues all too frequently in our day. In just the last century, three young women died martyrs for purity, preferring innocence—which meant death—to forced entry to their garden sanctuary.)

Joseph, turn away from your pleasure garden to Mary's garden, where you will find peace and light and true personhood. Call upon Our Lady, the New Eve, for assistance. She is the one who crushes the head of the serpent through her Son, as foretold by God to the serpent in Genesis 3:15: "I will put enmity between you and the woman, and between your off-spring and hers; he will strike at your head, while you strike at his heel." Mary is the New Eve whose son Jesus Christ defeats the devil. Pray to Our Lady. She will lead you to Jesus.

Be assured of my prayer for you, particularly at the holy sacrifice of the Mass, where we are most intimately united in the Mystical Body of Christ.

In Immaculate Heart of Our Lady of Mt. Carmel,

Fr. Terry

PS:

—Protect your garden and others by practicing custody of your eyes and imagination.

—Develop self-mastery by fasting from food and from other good pleasures.

—Conform your will to Christ by denying yourself!

3

To: **Joseph**

Date: **August 28—St. Augustine**

Re: **CONVERSION AND CONFESSION**

Dear Joseph,

Pardon the delay in responding to your e-mail, but I have been swamped with the work of the new semester. You wrote about your frustration in repeatedly confessing the same sins over and over: pornography, lust, masturbation. You wonder when those temptations will go away and when you'll stop acting on them. You say that your thoughts about your new colleague Lisa continue to be an occasion of lust. Since you've actually met her and exchanged a few words in passing, your nocturnal fantasies about her have increased. These exchanges with her were not heart to heart, you explain, because you feel a bit nervous around her as a result of your physical attraction to her and your guilty conscience in lusting after her.

I commend you for your sensitivity of conscience and for seeking out the sacrament of reconciliation, but in regard to your question about freedom from repeated sins, I want to know, what is the disposition of your heart when going to confession? What kind of contrition do you have? Do you *really* not want to commit these sins again?

As we mature from boys to men and grow into an adult faith, we begin to move from imperfect to perfect contrition. So often, a person can confess a sin, particularly a recurrent sin, with a contrition that does not reach beyond himself. This kind of contrition is ultimately just a feeling that I have sinned against *myself* and who I want to be; I feel guilt and shame because my actions and thoughts break a commandment or rule. This imperfect contrition is better than no contrition at all, but Jesus calls us to move to a deeper and more perfect contrition.

Do you go to confession with the firm purpose to amend your life, that you will never commit this sin again? I *will not* sin again. So often instead, our mindset is unreflective: "I will *try* not to do this again." Such a slogan is already an excuse waiting to be applied to the next temptation. Your whole self is not engaged. You have not changed your mind or purpose. You will *try* not to let your eyes linger on women's bodies; you will *try* to avoid certain websites; you will *try* to avoid certain cable channels. Where is the conviction in *try*? Where is the transformation? Where is the desire to do good? When you make a firm purpose of amendment, you make an act of faith and hope about the future and freedom from this sin. Your resolution is to say in your heart something like, I *will never* visit pornographic web sites. I *will only* watch television shows or movies that enhance my ability to be chaste. I *will avoid* internet sites, television, and movies that are occasions of sin, occasions in which I would be tempted to sin. But getting rid of vice and growing in virtue is not instantaneous. It is a journey, often long and arduous. So, do not despair with repeated failure. God's love and mercy for you abounds. He knows you more intimately than you do yourself. Jesus Christ is divine mercy, and he wept over the sins of Jerusalem.

Joseph, have you ever wept for your sins? Is confession mostly in the realm of a merely intellectual understanding of sin, or does it reach into your heart? Do you take seriously and understand the reality of sin? Sin is not so much a crime, a broken law, as it is a betrayal or denial of one you love, of the One who is Love. True, perfect contrition repents of the relationship you have broken with God.

Think about relationships you have with friends and family. Have you ever met someone who inspired you to change the way you live? Someone so thankful and gracious that you mourn your envy? Someone so patient that you mourn your wrath? Someone so noble in speech that you mourn your profanity? Someone so generous that you mourn your greed? Someone so chaste and pure that you mourn your lust and infidelity?

"The time has come and the kingdom of God is close at hand. Repent, and believe in the good news" (Mark 1:15). Such are the first words of Jesus in Mark's Gospel. *Repent.* In Greek, the imperative *metanoiete* means "change your mind or purpose." This change is not something as superfluous as turning down a friend's invitation and then later telling him, "I've changed my mind. I'll go with you." No, *metanoia* is a fundamental, radical, earth-shaking moment of insight and transformation. One's life is never the same afterward. *Metanoia* is the apostles' leaving everything behind because Jesus has captured their hearts: "At once they left their nets and followed him" (Mark 1:18). Their purpose and mind are irrevocably transformed by their encounter with Jesus. *Metanoia* is St. Peter falling to his knees and saying, "Leave me, Lord; I am a sinful man" (Luke 5:8). *Metanoia* is the sinful woman in Luke's Gospel whose tears fall on the feet of Jesus: "she wiped them away with her hair; then she covered his feet with kisses and anointed them" (Luke 7:45-47).

Today, we celebrate the memorial of St. Augustine, a man who long preferred sin to grace lest he have to change his life. In his autobiography, *The Confessions*, Augustine writes about his conversion and baptism as an adult. Outside of marriage, he lives with a woman and has a child, and as he is approaching his decisive moment of conversion, he prays to God, "Give me chastity...but not yet." He is close to conversion, but he holds back: "I could not reach out to it or grasp it, because I held back from the step by which I should die to death and become alive to life." He falls to the ground under a fig tree and cries, "How long shall I go on saying 'tomorrow, tomorrow'? Why not now? Why not make an end of my ugly sins at this moment?"

Repentance is knowing that sin is a betrayal or denial of the one you love—a betrayal of your very identity as one made in the image of God. Sin is the betrayal of Judas and the denial of Peter. Every temptation is a temptation to deny who you are and to whom you belong. The devil tempted Jesus by playing upon his identity. "If you are the Son of God," he said, then turn rocks into bread or throw yourself off the pinnacle of the temple. But Jesus does not abandon his humanity nor his union with the Father. He knows who he is and remains faithful to his identity and his communion with the Father in the Holy Spirit.

The devil tempts us also to deny and betray our true relationship to God and his Church. Peter wept after his denial of Jesus because he knew he had just betrayed the bond of friendship; he denied he ever knew Jesus. After Peter denied Jesus three times, only Luke's Gospel reports that Peter and Jesus were able to see each other: "And the Lord turned and looked at Peter. And Peter remembered the word of the Lord, how he had said to him, 'Before the cock crows today, you will deny me three times.' And he went out and wept bitterly" (Luke 22:61-62). The eyes of Peter and the Lord met in a tacit *cor ad cor loquitur* that seared Peter's unfaithful heart, and he wept. Denial. Betrayal. Peter had feared for his own life, that he too would be seized and condemned to death. In his denial of Christ, Peter pushed away his master and clung to himself.

Peter was forgiven for his sin by the risen Lord, three times professing his love—once for each denial—but on that Holy Thursday evening, Peter wept for his sin. Did he remember the first time he met this man from Nazareth, when Jesus told him to put out into deep water? Did he remember walking on water with the Lord and then sinking for lack of faith? Did he remember the Transfiguration on Mt. Tabor? Did he remember the feeding of the multitudes and the raising of Jairus's daughter, the widow of Nain's son, and Lazarus from the dead? Yet Peter preferred his own mortal life to union with Christ, and he wept when he recognized the magnitude of that sin. If you don't take your sin seriously enough, it is because you don't take your love of Christ seriously enough.

JOSEPH, THE TIME has come to make a decision. Christ's victory on the cross has set you free. You now live in the freedom of the Spirit; why do you so often seek to return to the prison of sin? You should flee from sin as if your life depended on it, for it does. I know that sin can be so familiar and comfortable. After years in prison, freedom's newness can challenge us. We fear the freedom of grace and can so easily turn back to the sin that we know. Did not the Israelites long for the familiar slavery of Egypt rather than confront the unknown of desert freedom and hope of the Promised Land?

Unlearn your old ways. Repent. The Kingdom is at hand. Turn away from the devil and follow the Lord. A man cannot serve two masters. Joseph, sins are not mere external actions and disembodied thoughts. They form—or rather *de*form—us. If you steal once, you are a person who has stolen. If you keep stealing again and again, you become a thief. In Tolkien's *Lord of the Rings*, the creature Gollum was once a hobbit-like person. He found a magical ring that made him invisible and used it for evil and malice. Over hundreds of years, he became a deformed creature, a skulking despiser of light and goodness.

Our sins are like the ring. Our desire for that ring, and our consent to wearing it slowly deforms us. Sin becomes habitual. Joseph, you must not put on the ring of lust and self-pleasure. It will destroy you. Instead, you must destroy it and be free of it. The ring may be precious to you; you may be accustomed to its luster and shape and feel on your finger. It's familiar, and you enjoy it. But in your heart, you also know that the ring is evil, that it is corrupting, that in wearing it you serve the Evil One.

That knowledge fills you with remorse and sends you to confession, but, because you have not tried to destroy the ring, you soon return to those sins. Overthrow the demon of lust. Fight it and kill it, which means part of you must die. Flee the dark land, and do not look back. Make for the blessed realm of the Kingdom, the land of purity. Breathe the fresh air of grace. Let your lungs fill with the breath of the Holy Spirit, transforming your heart into the likeness of Christ's.

This sanctification is your transformation; you become a new creation. You become not someone who tells the truth once in a while; you become a truthful man. You become not someone who is brave here and there; you become a courageous man. You become not someone who fasts from desires occasionally; you become a temperate man. You do not simply do good; you become a good man. Lust has no more place in you than darkness has in light.

Are you ready to destroy the ring? Are you ready to serve only Christ? Are you ready to leave behind lust—forever? Like Augustine, you seem to plead, "Tomorrow...tomorrow I will be good. Tomorrow I will change." Is it always tomorrow with you? The seed of the word of the Kingdom falls in your heart today—not tomorrow—and what environment does it find? Is your heart a stony path, a rocky, dry land, full of thorns and briars and brambles? Or is it a rich, loamy soil that supports a Garden of Eden paradise hospitable to and delighting in the Word of God? How do you prepare your heart today to receive the seed of the Word of the Kingdom? You will not change your ways, you will not have perfect contrition, and you will not weep for your sins until you know the goodness and beauty of the God whom you betray with those sins.

YEARS AGO, I saw a movie called *Moulin Rouge* in which the main character sings of his love for a woman. He is a writer and poet; she is a dancer and prostitute, and he seeks to raise her from that life to a fully human life. He sings out the window, and his words light up the city of Paris below. The camera focuses on her face in response to the beauty of his song and the love that generates it—which is fitting because the face portrays our personhood and humanity. I was captivated by the light in his eyes, the joy on his face, as he sang to win her heart. Love as gift of self.

This scene is also an image of God's love for sinful humanity. The prophets compared the relationship between God and Israel to that between a husband and his adulteress wife. God continues to love Israel despite her sins and yearns for her to open her heart and live in the freedom and truth that God offers. Nothing can separate us from God's love. No matter how great our sin, God loves us and pursues us.

Do you experience his love—are you moved by the beauty

of the One who wants you? Are you so moved by that beauty that you change your life, that you let God's Spirit burn in your heart, that you sing for joy in return? Is your heart open to participate in God's love song for you in Christ? Your response to this love song is to become one with Christ and all those whom he calls. Through baptism, you enter into the life of Christ and become a member of his Body, the Church. You belong to him. You belong to one another.

May the glory of God set your heart on fire as it did Augustine. *Metanoiete.* Repent! Joseph, "let us lay aside every encumbrance of sin which clings to us and persevere in running the race which lies ahead; let us keep our eye fixed on Jesus, who inspires and perfects our faith" (Heb. 12:1). St. Paul wrote to the Colossians,

> Since you have been brought back to true life with Christ, you must look for the things that are in heaven, where Christ is, sitting at God's right hand. Let your thoughts be on heavenly things, not on the things that are on the earth. . . . That is why you must kill everything in you that belongs only to earthly life: fornication, impurity. . . . You have stripped off your old behavior with your old self, and you have put on a new self which will progress toward true knowledge the more it is renewed in the image of its creator (3:1-10).

Joseph, give thanks to God for your vocation, your calling to be a Christian, a follower of Christ, to live in union with the Father through the Holy Spirit, and to live in communion with all those who have been baptized and share the life of the sacraments, prayer, and service in communion with the pope and bishops. Reject Satan and all his empty promises. Remember your baptismal identity and promises. Repent of your sin and confess it in the sacrament of reconciliation. Be sanctified in and by the Holy Spirit. Pray with St. Augustine in his words:

> Breathe in me, thou Holy Spirit,
> that I may think what is holy.
> Move me, thou Holy Spirit,
> that I may do what is holy.
> Attract me, thou Holy Spirit,
> that I may love what is holy.
> Strengthen me, thou Holy Spirit,
> that I may guard what is holy.
> Guard me, thou Holy Spirit,
> that I may never lose what is holy.

Be assured of my prayer for you, particularly at the holy sacrifice of the Mass, where we are most intimately united in the Mystical Body of Christ.

In the freedom of conversion and life in the crucified Lord,

Fr. Terry

PS:

—Trust in God's mercy and go to confession regularly.

—Renew your baptismal promises every morning and examine your conscience every night.

—Bring your heart with its burden of sin to the Sacred Heart of Christ!

4

To: Joseph

Date: **28 September—St. Wenceslaus**

Re: GROWING IN KINGLY WISDOM

Dear Joseph,

In the silent hours of night, I left the mountain house of solitude to meet the holy darkness and await the dawn. With the soft light of the waning third-quarter moon, I followed the earthen path, soft with hemlock needles and the vanguard of autumn leaf fall, as it climbed beside the cobblestone stream until I reached my destination. On an aromatic blanket of gentle evergreen needles I sat down beneath a sentinel long standing at its post. This eastern hemlock has kept watch at over four centuries of daybreaks on this mountain edge, where the guiding banks of the spring-fed stream halt and let it fall twenty feet to the plunge pool below. The break in the forest on this east-facing slope of the mountain allows an unobstructed view of the heavens and the approaching dawn.

As I sat amidst this plenitude of Creation, I knew myself

to be creature, and my being ached to worship the Creator. Jacob, the grandson of Abraham, had a dream in which he saw a stairway (or ladder) joining earth and heaven, with angels ascending and descending upon it (Gen. 28:12). In this contemplation of Creation, I climbed upon the first rung of Jacob's Ladder. The entire world of Creation, the sensible world, is before us as a mirror in which to see the footprints of the Trinity. St. Bonaventure thought that Creation, seen properly with the intellect, is a rung of Jacob's Ladder by which "we shall mount up to God, the Supreme Creator." Though kin of all Creation, we are given a kingly responsibility to rule it, following the model of Christ the King who is the Wisdom of God.

Through the Word of God all of Creation came to be, and wisdom allows us to understand the Word through creatures, including ourselves. Without this wisdom, our governance as kings becomes tyrannical, capricious, and utilitarian. This not only affects our relationship to Creation but also affects our understanding and governance of ourselves as human creatures. How do we learn to read, speak, and understand this language of Creation, and especially about ourselves as human creatures? How do we ascend Jacob's Ladder to the Creator?

After encountering the dawn this morning, I returned to the chapel and offered Mass on this feast of St. Wenceslaus, a young married king of Bohemia and martyr of the tenth century. King Wenceslaus is one of the few married saints on the liturgical calendar, yet the Church is composed predominantly of married men and women. How does the Church help form holy husbands and wives?

As MAN AND woman, our bodies speak a nuptial language of trinitarian love. Through our baptism, we enter into the life of Jesus Christ as priest, prophet, and king. We possess a royal power to order society, our families, and ourselves in holiness. With kingly governance and wisdom, we are to overcome the reign of sin in ourselves and to enter into that kingdom of truth, life, holiness, grace, justice, love, and peace.

Joseph, your e-mail—which I printed and brought with me to this mountain solitude—reveals a king who is governed more by passions than by reason. Instead of a King Wenceslaus, who ascends Jacob's Ladder and who humbly orders his life to the Trinity, you seem to be more like King David, governed by lust for Bathsheba bathing on the rooftop. My gladness at the good news of your newly developing relationship with Lisa is only equal to my disappointment and concern about it. The joy and excitement you have experienced these last three weeks since your first date poured off your e-mail and revealed the invigorating effect she has on you. Her presence stirs your heart to greater heights of awareness—particularly of her. As you admit, Lisa fills your thoughts; you call and text her every day, you want to be in her presence, you want to see her, you go over to her apartment, and you think about where to go and what to do with her.

These are the marks of a heart no longer focused solely on the self but on another person, yet I am concerned about the nature of your thoughts about her, how you talk to her, the nature of your conversations, and the decisions you make about how to encounter one another in and through your bodies. I am concerned about how kingly you are, about your personal integrity, about how you and Lisa help one another ascend the Ladder to and with God, and about your ability to comprehend the language of being man and woman.

As you note, these last three weeks with Lisa raise new questions and new temptations. You tell me that since developing this relationship with Lisa, your struggles with lust, pornography, and masturbation have actually increased. Now the effects of these sins have a direct impact on another person—now you may lead another person into sin to satisfy your lust. You describe how you desire her body. You are unsettled as you harbor and feed that desire. The power and intensity of such thoughts, reinforced by pleasurable, yet impure, actions can blind you to the truth of human sexuality and relationships.

Lust blinds your mind, which then, as Aquinas rightly observes, "excludes almost entirely the knowledge of spiritual things." You become more and more like King Herod Antipas, whose lust for Salome blinded him to truth and goodness. He could not govern himself; he made rash promises to Salome that would cost John the Baptist his life. He engulfed himself in an imaginary world where he could be with Salome: an illusory world of selfish sensual pleasure without responsibility. Likewise, David's lust for Bathsheba isolated him from clear thought and responsibility. He committed adultery, betrayed the covenant with God, and caused the death of her husband in battle.

Joseph, all that we have discussed about virtue, personhood, character, discipleship, prayer, and holiness is at a crossroads. Judgment that was once swift and clear becomes impaired in a mind blinded by sexual desire. Reason is abandoned to the appetites, and the clarity and sharpness of truth is dulled. What's more, the encapsulating bubble in which lovers often dwell can dampen the words of others and isolate its dwellers from other relationships. Life in that world seems fresh and new and intimate. Each person is the desire of the other. The occupants of the bubble are compelled to maintain it, for within it they feel refreshed and loved and understood. In the bubble, there are no responsibilities or difficulties. It is a world without suffering and an escape from demands and struggles. The bubble is a world without the Cross.

This bubble often plays a part in adultery and the breaking of vows, whether of married couples or of religious and priests. A husband meets a woman at work to whom he feels a certain attraction. Instead of tending the boundaries of his garden even more vigilantly, he deliberately begins talking with her on a regular basis. He enjoys her company and the attention she gives him. This may occur even with men whose marriages are going well, but the situation is even more pronounced if any stress or difficulty exists at home with his wife. The bubble starts to form. The husband does not tell his wife about this new relationship. Truth begins to be suppressed and confined. The conversations with the co-worker increase; the privacy of e-mail and texts allows communications that would be impossible in public conversation; opportunities to be together are created and taken. Inside the swelling bubble, the husband finds a world in which the difficulties at home with his wife and children are forgotten. The woman at work becomes the focus of his attention. He feels a freshness and vitality he has not known for years. What he knew to be un-thinkable on his wedding day, and even after years of mar-riage, suddenly does not seem so wrong.

The bubble must be protected from popping, which would exacerbate the pain the husband is avoiding and from which he is escaping. Lunches are extended. The meetings become more clandestine and prolonged. Compassion and yearnings are translated into touches. Touches intensify. Within the bub-ble, the touches seem good and nourishing. The ugliness of adultery is muted and dulled by the pleasure and comfort and seeming good that comes from the new relationship. He can talk with the other woman in a way he does not with his wife. He feels a closeness and trust. His conscience tells him that what he is doing is sinful, but the bubble around his heart numbs the sting. He goes to confession, yet with imperfect contrition. He does not really want to give up this bubble life. Can he not have both? His wife and the co-worker? The hus-band wants to avoid the difficulty of fidelity. He wants to es-cape and remain in the world he and the co-worker create—a world where they exist for one another. All other responsibil-ities and concerns are sacrificed to sustain the illusory world.

Although it is not adulterous, your account of your de-veloping relationship with Lisa bears the marks of bubble initiation. After your initial chance encounters with her, you started to actively cross paths with her. Conversations and meetings increased and became more flirtatious. You started to text one another during the day and after work. As the bubble thickened, it began to muffle the voice of virtue; Lisa became more and more the subject of your lustful imaginings, and you started to enclose her in a world of your own creation. Bodily desires for her intensified and bore fruit in solitary pleasure. Part of your desire for forming an exclusive relationship with her is caught up in your lust for her.

A week after your first date, you and Lisa went out to dinner, a date that ended early in the morning with unexpected intense exploratory touching at her apartment and left you wanting more. What you once held firm about boundaries is now cast into doubt. The bubble forms around you as your body roars in a language that hampers lucid thought. After a few more nights of touching and exploration, you call into question the validity of limits to what seems good and relationally enhancing. Though you've not had intercourse, you write about the intimacy of bodily self-revelation to one another. The intensity of knowing one another bodily, the trust to reveal oneself to another, and the pleasure it all brings make you wonder if having any limits is just prudish.

Joseph, as you have been discerning your vocation to marriage, you've been firm in your intention to remain a virgin until then. The present is a preparation for that future goal. Like many men your age, you struggle with chastity and purity and how to govern your sexual desires. You've grown in self-mastery over the last couple months, but now in three weeks, your goal is called into question. You wonder how wrong premarital sex can really be. Perhaps, you suggest, virginity was a premature goal, based on insufficient experience and knowledge. You didn't realize how intimate and intense bodily sharing with a woman could be. Chastity and virginity now seem bland.

In this bubble you do not look upon Lisa's body or your own with wisdom but with lust, and you enclose yourselves in a world of your own creation that is intentionally exclusive of God the Creator.

Joseph, you must *pierce the bubble*. Your confusion calls for clarity. On the one hand, you ask, "What is wrong with such a relationship when every aspect of it feels good? Is it hurting anyone?" On the other hand, you write of your uneasiness with where you think this relationship seems to be heading and of your doubts about whether you are building a true friendship with Lisa or just using one another for sexual pleasure. In college, you did not participate in the hookup culture, but you were very much aware of it; what you are describing seems to me like an extended hookup rather than an authentic friendship. I want to show you a better way. I want to help you pierce the bubble by placing sexual love in the pure, keen, radiant light of truth—the truth of marriage and the inherent nuptial dimension of our bodies. I want to show you how to be a wise king.

MY FIRST QUESTION for you is this: "Are you ready to be a father?" The bubble quivers at that question, for it introduces an element of responsibility to its carefree and untroubled environment. The word "father" introduces a third party to the bubble that wants to be just for two. In your conflicted imaginings about sex with Lisa, however, you said that part of the temptation comes from knowing that she is on the Pill. In the hookup culture, children are not welcome. You desire Lisa and her body and sexual pleasure, but you have no interest in another human being who would fundamentally reorient your life. The bubble's isolation from responsibility is exposed. It creates an imaginary world where sexual relations exclude the procreative possibility. The man and woman remain alone with themselves in exclusive bliss.

But this world is false. *Real* sexual love is the fullest expression of the mystery of human communion, in which a man and a woman say to each other, in the nuptial language of the body, "I want to have a child with you." The love they have for one another yearns for and is naturally directed toward their—together—loving a third person. Love between just two people is incomplete in that they do not together give their love away to someone else, such as a child.

Together, the Father and the Son love the Holy Spirit, who proceeds from them both. When a husband and wife love one another, their spousal and conjugal love is directed toward and embodied in the procreation of a third whom they can love together.

The union of their bodies is also an expression of their desire for one another—and *only* one another. Fidelity. Sex with strangers or prostitutes, hookup sexual encounters, sex with someone who is not your spouse—these are all unitive and bonding in a limited sense, but the "partners" involved do not intend the lifelong exclusivity pointed to by the language of their bodily union. Only the vowed commitment to lifelong fidelity of husband and wife in marriage actualizes the lifelong fidelity expressed by sexual union. Men and women are ordered to one another, and only as a unitive, complementary couple can they, through their procreative organs, reach the end for which they are ordered. By its nature the sexual act is ordered to procreation, whether or not the conception of a child will take place. Children, furthermore, have both the right and the need to grow up in a stable family with a mother and father. Thus, lifelong fidelity between a husband and wife is a good in itself that serves the good of raising children to whom the spouses give their love. Finally, sexual love deepens the bond between man and woman. They grow in knowledge and love of one another.

The lifelong fidelity of marital love between husband and wife is a covenant that is an image of God's indissoluble covenant with his people. God espouses himself forever to his people in steadfast love and mercy (Hos. 2:19). Isaiah tells the people of Israel that they are the wife, and their Creator and Redeemer is their husband (Isa. 54:5-6).

Marriage is the only true setting for this sexual love. Marriage is the grammar that makes the nuptial language of sexual expression true, coherent, and authentic. Sex is inherently a human personal sharing, an encounter in which husband and wife expose themselves and give themselves completely to one another; it is a total gift of self in which they are open to the completion of shared love with a third.

Sex outside of marriage betrays both our trinitarian image and the image of God's covenant with us. It also falsifies human expression and communion. How will your relationship with Lisa prepare yourself for the splendor and responsibility of covenantal married love, for that mystery of profound interpersonal communion? How will you learn to be authentic so that you can fluently speak the noble nuptial language of bodily love? Will you govern your desires and your being with kingly wisdom? Will you ascend Jacob's Ladder and see with the wise eyes of faith the sacramental dimension of our identity as creatures?

JOSEPH, THE SEXUAL love of a Christian husband and wife speaks not only about their human covenant, but about Christ's redemptive love for the Church. When Christian spouses become one flesh, their bodies speak a language that signifies the oneness of Christ with his Body the Church: "This is a great mystery, but I speak in reference to Christ and the Church" (Eph. 5:32). The consummation of the Christian husband and wife in sexual love is not a mere instinct of biology, and it is not only human love and communion; it is a sacramental sign of that great mystery of Christ and the Church. And as with all the sacraments, it is ordered toward our redemption and salvation.

Jesus Christ himself is Jacob's Ladder, uniting humankind with God, humanity with divinity. Upon him even the angels of God ascend and descend (John 1:51). Joseph, draw near to Christ and ascend upon him so that you may grow in kingly wisdom. Ponder anew the dignity and meaning of marriage and sexual love in light of Christ. How is your relationship with Lisa commensurate with the mystery of marital sexual love? You are not just a man and a woman of flesh; you are beings oriented to the divine mystery of love. Baptized into the life of Christ the King, govern your desires concerning Lisa in holiness and justice.

Be assured of my prayer for you and Lisa, particularly at the holy sacrifice of the Mass, where we are most intimately united in the Mystical Body of Christ.

In the kingship of Christ as we ascend Jacob's Ladder,

Fr. Terry

PS:

—Defuse lustful thoughts by asking yourself, "Am I ready to be a father?"

—Don't keep your relationships hidden in a bubble. Seek the counsel of trusted friends about them.

—Govern your desires and passions with wisdom in the kingship of Christ!

To: **Joseph**

Date: **15 October—St. Teresa of Avila**

Re: **LOVING GOD WITH YOUR**

WHOLE HEART

Dear Joseph,

May the Spirit of freedom and love be with you. Now
that I have finished grading exams and our mid-semes-
ter break has begun, I can devote time to your latest e-mail.

I commend your decision to pray about your relationship
with Lisa and how to talk with her about how you relate
to one another. You like her, but you also acknowledge that
the physical dimension seems to dominate your desires and
interactions. Develop the friendship dimension by engaging
her person. Be with her, talk with her, and share activities
that engage your hearts and minds without bodily passion
and sexual touching. Show her what a man of God is like,
Joseph!

In asking me about yourself, about your relationship with

Lisa, and about sexual desires, you also wondered how priests and nuns live out their celibacy. I want to share my personal reflections on this with you.

Contrary to celibate love being foreign to many people's experience, I contend that everyone, whether married or not, is to have a celibate heart that loves God alone. Priests and religious, of course, are called to a special kind of single-hearted intimacy with God. Today's saint, Teresa of Avila, was a Carmelite nun and mystic who lived in sixteenth-century Spain. Her chaste life and spiritual writings reveal how the human person is sanctified and transformed by the power of the Holy Spirit. When we are receptive to the presence of God, he draws us into a union with himself, which, as Teresa declares, is "above all earthly joys, above all delights, above all consolations." The celibacy practiced by priests and religious reminds *all* of us that our human nature was created for communion with the Trinity. Every person is to have a celibate heart.

For my part, I love being celibate. This surprises a lot of people. I haven't conducted a scientific investigation, but I think that most people outside the Church (and many within!) do not understand celibacy. For example, shortly before I entered the seminary, I attended the wedding of my friend Carl. At the rehearsal dinner, at which I was the only Catholic, another guest was perplexed to learn that I would be entering the seminary in a few months and embarking upon a life of celibacy. He thought that everyone needed a sexual companion, and if I couldn't have a wife I should have someone to keep me "company." Celibacy was foreign to his vision of life. Another friend simply could not comprehend that someone could forego sex and still find life enjoyable.

Both of those responses were rooted in the common myth that to be celibate is to be lonely. But the loneliness of celibacy is no greater than the loneliness of marriage. At our core, *everyone* is lonely. In the depth of our hearts exists a loneliness that cannot be cured by any created thing or person. Human beings are incomplete. We must eat and drink to survive. We are not self-sufficient. As much as we yearn for immortality, we are mortal and will die. We are not the cause of our own being. We know ourselves as male or female and recognize that we are not the whole story; we are incomplete, and we may think that marriage solves this incompleteness.

Most people in the world are married or will be married. Married love is the content of songs, movies, books, novels, plays, and musicals. Even divine revelation in Scripture uses the image of marriage to help us understand God. God is the husband, and Israel is his spouse. In the New Covenant, the Church is the bride and Christ the bridegroom. Our lives as humans are inherently nuptial. But there is a danger. By thinking that their husband or wife will remove their loneliness and bring them fulfillment, some married people confuse their spouse with God.

Our popular culture promotes this idolatrous myth. I remember a movie about a married couple whose young children die in a car accident. Shortly after that, the husband dies, and the wife, in her despair, kills herself. The husband abandons his life in heaven to seek his wife amidst the dark underworld. Upon finding her and rescuing her, they return to heaven, but their stay is short. They abandon heaven and communion with their children to return to earth to fall in love with each other all over again. Heaven, it seems, was an inferior substitute for their earthly marital love. They sought an eternal relationship of just two people without desire of anyone else. In a common sentiment among lovers, they effectively said to one another, "You complete me."

These stories reveal a poor understanding of the human person. In reality, we have an inherent loneliness, an emptiness that only God can fill. Only he can complete us. St. Augustine, in the first paragraph of *The Confessions,* speaks to this inner insatiable loneliness: "Our hearts are restless, Lord, until they rest in thee." We are forever lonely on this side of heaven, until we come face to face with God in the kingdom.

A common image of married love is of a man and a woman face to face; they gaze at one another in a deep, interpenetrating intimacy. Friendship, by contrast, is often depicted with the two friends side by side. In the kingdom, we will *all* be side by side, together facing God, like worshiping at Mass. In the Gospels, Jesus reveals that there will be no marriage in the kingdom of heaven. He confronts the Sadducees, who did not believe in angels or resurrection. They pose a trick question involving a woman who had been married seven times, asking Jesus whose wife she would be in heaven.

Jesus responds, "You are misled because you do not know Scripture or the power of God. At the resurrection they neither marry nor are given in marriage but are like the angels in heaven" (Matt. 22:29-30). Angels are purely spiritual creatures and are, therefore, celibate by nature. And so all hearts will be "celibate" in heaven—living in single-hearted intimacy with

God. Celibate priests and religious on earth are visible signs of that heavenly reality.

All of us, whether married or celibate, must a celibate heart in that our deepest desire should be for God. Jesus commands us to love God—not our spouse, children, or friends—with *all* of our heart, soul, and mind (Matt. 22:37). I am still learning how to do that. It takes a lifetime, and the process will only be complete in heaven.

Most people look at celibates as strange or at celibacy as unnatural. It *is* un-natural in the sense that it is super-natural; it belongs to the divine realm of seeking union with God. Henri Nouwen, great spiritual writer of the late twentieth century, wrote, "Celibacy is a part of Christian man. Celibacy is not a state reserved for a few, but . . . celibacy and being empty for God has a very deep meaning in a marriage relationship . . . A celibate priest or religious is only a visible sign, a visible display or a reality which can be found in every man's life. A celibate man or woman is called to protect and to understand loneliness as a basic human condition in the life of every Christian." Everybody is lonely, and our completion is found in God alone. Married love is not intended to take away loneliness, but husbands and wives should be ministering to one another to help each other find God and give his or her heart fully to him.

I love being celibate. A favorite movie of mine, *Chariots of Fire,* tells the story of Eric Liddell, a sprinter who competed at the 1924 Summer Olympics. He says humbly, "God made me fast, and when I run I feel his pleasure." When I live and love celibately, *I* feel God's pleasure. Celibacy does not thwart my human development or diminish my passion or dampen my love. To the contrary, celibacy is an ardent expression of the torrent of God's love.

ST. IRENAEUS, A second-century bishop and martyr, rightly understood and proclaimed the truth of the human person when he wrote that "the glory of God is a living man; and the life of man consists in beholding God." The human person is a single integrated whole of body and soul who is the image of God. The *image* is not just a part of man, such as mind, intellect, or reason, but it is the whole person. We are the *likeness* of God when we are united with the Holy Spirit. The Spirit forms us into spiritual men and women. In baptism and confirmation, we receive the Holy Spirit, who makes of us a new creation. We become his temples. We enter into the very divine life of Christ and the Holy Trinity. Without the Spirit we remain carnal men, who, as St. Irenaeus describes, "reject the Spirit's counsel, are slaves of fleshly lusts, lead lives contrary to reason, and without restraint plunge headlong into their own desires." The complete man—the human person intimately permeated by the Spirit—dwells in the freedom of grace.

Celibacy is an eschatological sign. The Greek word *eschaton* means the end, the last, the final age. Theologically, *eschaton* is the completion and fulfillment of our lives in communion with the Father through the Son in the Holy Spirit. Celibacy lives in the present what we anticipate in the end, when God will be all in all. Celibacy is not a mere ascetical program and renunciation of marriage; it is an eschatological vocation. It is a life of consecration to God. Celibacy bears visible witness to our embodied vocation and to the completion—or perfection—of our life in Christ. Foremost, we are celibate because of Jesus Christ.

Celibacy is not a denial of human nature but a consecration that points to the *fullness* of our human nature. It is not an escape from relationships and intimacy but a call to the greatest and most intense intimacy and communion with others. It is not a denigration of marriage but the eschatological sign of mystical union with God and with the Church. It is not a fear of or dismissal of the body but a joyful delight in bodily existence. Celibacy does not diminish human love but transforms it, purifies it, and orders it properly with the love of God.

At the heart of celibacy, which will order all other human loves, is the love of God. The celibate heart sings Psalm 63 without ceasing:

> God, you are my God, for you I long;
> for you my soul is thirsting.
> My body pines for you
> like a dry, weary land without water.
> So I gaze on you in the sanctuary
> to see your strength and your glory.
> For your love is better than life.
> My lips will speak your praise.
> So I will bless you all my life;
> in your name I will lift up my hands.
> My soul shall be filled as with a banquet,

my mouth shall praise you with joy.
On my bed I remember you.
On you I muse through the night.
For you have been my help;
In the shadow of your wings I rejoice.
My soul clings to you,
my right hand holds you fast.

THE CHURCH OF Santa Maria della Vittoria in Rome con-
tains Bernini's marble sculpture of St. Teresa in ecstasy. He
expressed magnificently St. Teresa's mystical experience of
divine love. St. Teresa writes of the angelic transverberation—
that is, the piercing of her heart with a fiery spear: "In his
hands I saw a long golden spear and at the end of the iron tip
I seemed to see a point of fire. When he drew it out . . . he left
me completely afire with a great love for God. The pain was
so sharp that it made me utter several moans; and so excessive
was the sweetness caused me by this intense pain that one
can never wish to lose it, nor will one's soul be content with
anything less than God."

I've had my own experience of the purity of God's love
that opened up my heart after years of hard-heartedness to
the freedom of celibate love. Jesus spoke about the disciples'
hardness of heart (in Greek, *sklerokardia*). Ezekiel prophesied
about God's removing the heart of stone from his people and
giving them hearts of flesh (36:26). When I was about your
age, I described in my journal the experience of forgiveness

and a new heart: in this openness to God, I laughed in ecstatic joy as God poured his love upon my heart as lava that seeps into the thick, impenetrable shell—*sklerokardia*—encasing my heart. Liquid fire burned and penetrated all in its path. My heart of stone, once solid and impervious, melted into living flesh. A once solid mass became a spacious cavern, a chamber of light and golden fire. Expansive rooms and great halls opened up from a golden torrent of divine grace. The debris of darkness and sin could not withstand this deluge of holiness sweeping down in a frenzy of sanctified might. I breathed in the purity of the Spirit. My lungs expanded. I soared in delight, weightless, unencumbered by sin. My mind saw with keenness.

I want to engage the world in this freedom. I feel the Son's mission: "I have come to bring fire to the earth, and how I wish it were blazing already" (Luke 12:49). In the freedom and pure love of the Spirit, Christ encountered human hearts. *Cor ad cor loquitur.* God came seeking the hearts of men and women to set their souls on fire. Jesus the Christ, the Son of Mary, the Son of God, came to announce the kingdom of God. He entered into our human lives to reveal his Father's love. Love met Peter and Andrew and called them to be fishers of men. Love met Mary Magdalene and freed her from seven demons. Love awoke the daughter of Jairus from the sleep of death. Love healed lepers. Love fed the hungry. Love made the deaf hear and the blind see. Love met the impure of heart and body—tax collectors and prostitutes—and purified them. Love held innocent children and comforted widows. Love sought out the most recalcitrant and sick. Love transformed the world. Love poured himself out on a cross that all might be with the Father in the Holy Spirit. Love sought nothing for himself. Love unites us all together as vine and branches. Love became human and revealed to us our true selves and the truth of God.

Do you know the look of Love? Do you know Love's touch, compassion, mercy, and freedom? Celibacy is nothing less than a call to love as Love. Celibate love desires to burn with divine freedom and purity, to be a fiery witness to the mission, to the blessed realm where all hearts turn to the Tri-une God. Celibate love is a burning love of the Crucified. St. Teresa teaches, "Fix your eyes on the Crucified and every-thing will become small for you." The celibate heart glows with the living flame of Love, consumed with desire to share the freedom and sacrifice and magnanimity of Christ's love with others.

Love of Love makes us better lovers. The closer we are to God, the more we catch fire, the more freely, maturely, and humanly we love our brothers and sisters—we who share the same Father. "You have put into my heart a marvelous love for the faithful ones who dwell in your land" (Ps. 16). True celibacy glorifies God in the body and engages the bodily being of another in a manner that is holy and honorable. I delight in the truth of *cor ad cor loquitur*. Contrary to worldly wisdom, which worships before the altar of Eros as the pinnacle of human self-satisfaction and fulfillment, celibate love burns with divine love—*agape*. Jesus Christ transforms the world because of the love of God that he reveals and gives to us.

Worldly wisdom cannot imagine a love that only gives

and does not need; cannot imagine a man who encounters a woman and does not desire to sleep with her; cannot imagine a man who gazes upon a woman, not with lustful fantasies, but with a purity that embraces her entire personhood and not merely her flesh. The height of celibacy is to love with the Sacred Heart of Christ. I feel the Lord's pleasure in the *agapic* encounter of another in my priestly celibacy as I forgive sins in the confessional. I see with *agapic* vision rather than erotic vision. I encounter another with freedom, not need; I encounter one's embodied personhood, not just one's flesh. I encounter another in Christ. In true priestly celibacy, I encounter another at the well of the Trinity, as Jesus encountered the Samaritan woman at Jacob's well.

Our beings are wells that, at their depth, rest in the fontal fullness of the Father. He is the life-giving source of all. He is the infinite ocean of love. Jesus comes to root us in this life-giving water so that we may drink deeply from it. He comes to slake our thirst with baptismal water: "Deep is calling on deep in the roar of waters: your torrents and all your waves swept over me" (Ps. 42). As a celibate priest, I delight to encounter people at the shore of that ocean. But this love Jesus brings is not just for vowed celibates. Mothers and fathers and grandparents are to have this love, to drink from this well of life-giving water. This fundamental love of God then forms and transforms all of their other loves: love of spouse, children, neighbor. You, too, are to have this single-hearted intimacy with God.

Joseph, you also have to know that true celibacy does not arise instantaneously when the vow of celibacy is professed.

It is a maturity and a capacity for relationships that requires human effort, coupled with God's grace, to bring to completion. Priests and all celibates must grow in personhood and virtue. The vow of celibacy does not automatically transform one into a chaste man without sin or the perfect man in union with God. Human formation never ends, and the most important element for the celibate, as for any Christian, is self-knowledge. St. Teresa of Avila writes, "Rather, let us strive to make more progress in self-knowledge, for in my opinion we shall never completely know ourselves if we don't strive to know God. By gazing at his grandeur, we get in touch with our own loneliness; by looking at his purity, we shall see our own filth; by pondering his humility, we shall see how far we are from being humble."

Celibacy is not the only route of holiness in relationships, but it is a truth about our union with God that justly orders all human relationships and our sexuality. The marital relationship of husband and wife must be rooted in each spouse's relationship with God. Celibacy, rather than being unnatural and irrelevant to humanity, is a universal truth—for the married, single, and avowed alike—about rooting our heart, soul, strength, mind, and sexual body in God. St. Paul writes to the Christians at Thessalonika about our embodied humanity and sexuality, "What God wants is for you all to be holy. He wants you to keep away from fornication, and each one of you to know how to use the body that belongs to him in way that is holy and honorable, not giving way to selfish lust like the pagans who do not know God" (1 Thess. 4:3-6).

Joseph, may the purity and freedom of the Holy Spirit

transform you into the spiritual man. Know of my prayers for you, especially in the holy sacrifice of the Mass.

In the fire of Christ's love,

Fr. Terry

PS:

—Pray Psalm 63 often.

—Get to know men and women who are vowed celibates.

—Love your neighbor with the Sacred Heart of Christ!

To: **Joseph**

Date: **November 1—All Saints**

Re: SURROUNDING YOURSELF WITH SAINTS

Dear Joseph,

B lessed be God in his saints! Today we celebrate the So-
lemnity of All Saints, which includes those canonized
by the Church and the much greater number known only to
God. St. Paul also called all those who are baptized into the
life of Christ "saints." A Christian believer in this world is a
saint, a *holy one*.

How amazing when we meet those who truly live a life in
Christ filled with God's Holy Spirit! These men and women
scale the heights of our human personhood. My soul delights
in your recent encounters with such saints. Your last e-mail
reveals that your heart knew and was moved by the purity
of holy friendship—that you experienced the truth of being
person. St. Thomas rightly describes a person as "that which is

most noble and most perfect in all of nature." Personhood is
that living image of the Trinity that is a capacity for love and
freedom and communion with others, and ultimately with
God, the Trinity of Persons. We discover and become truly
ourselves as persons by our whole-hearted openness to the
inexhaustible mystery of God.

What a gift you have received these last two weeks. Thanks
be to God for the communion of holiness you shared with
the Culross family, whose sanctity shines with a transfigur-
ing glow that drew you into their realm of blessedness. When
we're with people truly striving for holiness, it illumines our
minds and hearts with a standard by which we can gain insight into ourselves.

You write movingly of the encounter with the Culross
siblings, initially at your friend's wedding, where the oldest,
Pete, was the priest. His sisters Clare and Aggie along with
his brother Steve and his fiancée Marie provided the music;
then you spent time with them at the reception and the next
morning at the hotel. Your words and expressions reveal the
authenticity of an encounter with holiness—from the beauty
of the Mass, which was truly prayer and worship "in Spirit
and in truth," to the communion you shared with these saints.
Blessed be God. You also experienced why the Church holds
sacred music as the greatest and most treasured of all forms of
art. Sacred music transforms and elevates our prayer and draws
us into communion with one another and with God.

What made these two Masses, the nuptial Mass on Saturday afternoon and the Sunday Mass at the hotel, in your
own words, "the two most amazing and powerful Masses" you

have ever experienced, is the ecstasy of divine love. Theologian Hans Urs von Balthasar described our lives as a drama, "an exhilarating love story, in which divine love courts sinful humanity." You were brought close to the living flame of love. You experienced the noble splendor of the Church. The power and beauty of that weekend's experience was precisely the community of which you were a part and the communion you shared with those present. You participated in and with the Holy—the Holy Trinity and the holy people of God. You were in communion with the saints, the holy ones. You met the living stones of the Church, and you are a changed man.

You expressed a deep yearning to be in their company. You realized, just by being in their presence, that you could be better than you are, and it would seem so effortless, like when you watch an expert athlete perform. You recognized that your vision has been too dim, your heart too small, your mind too confused. Conversion exposes our prior lack of love.

As you reluctantly separated from the Culrosses and went to your hotel room, you were unable to sleep because you felt that you were floating—perhaps "soaring in bliss" would be more apt. "Blessed are the pure of heart, for they shall see God" (Matt. 5:8). Like Ebenezer Scrooge, you had a purgatorial night—not visited by ghosts but touched by grace and a longing to give yourself to Truth and Love. You expressed sorrow and shame about your relationship with Lisa, but that repentance was engulfed in a torrent of hope in which you saw the living answer of who you could be.

After just a few hours in the presence of the Culrosses, you knew that lust was a shadow that did not belong in the presence of their light. You let the images from the evening wash over you, images of true humanity and true community, images of the noble love of majestic beings united by their mutual love for one another in God: the music and voices at the wedding, the tender affection of Pete, Steve, Marie, Clare, and Aggie for each other; the glow on their faces; the lively light in their eyes; the seriousness of purpose in their bearing yet the levity of their movement and in their smiles; the graciousness of their responses to strangers, the measured words of conversation reflective of the import and gravity of human speech; the attentiveness and anticipation of another's needs; the beauty of virtue; the excellence of their talents—whether it be music, dance, or as you learned later, fencing. I would have enjoyed their dancing performance: Fr. Pete with Clare (who, you say, will be going to the convent next year) and Steve with Aggie—the mellifluous motion, masterful direction, strength and stamina, flowing and twirling dresses, dexterous throws and jumps, the familiarity and rapport, the confident yet delicate touch of hands, and the silent awe of the crowd.

It was a beauty of body that sang about spirit—a beauty that, in conjunction with all of who they are, expanded your lungs. Just to be in their presence was expansive.

I think what you experienced with these friends is the blessedness offered to every human person by the Blessed One. They are friends with one another because they are friends of God. I am glad that you have experienced the bliss of drawing near to the Holy One who calls all of us to a life of love with him. We are made in his triune image, to love one another in him. Pope St. John Paul II wrote that the Holy Spirit calls us to friendship in which "the transcendent 'depths of God' become . . . opened to participation on the part of man." The Dominican theologian Yves Congar reflected on the Holy Spirit, "Only God can lead us to his own sphere, his own inheritance, his own state of blessedness, and his own glory, which is himself. Only God, in other words, can make us act divinely." Your desire to be with and *like* the Culrosses is a desire for that ability to act divinely. God has created us in his triune image to be in relation with him and one another so that we might be holy and perfect as he is holy and perfect. But we can't do this on our own. We must open ourselves to the action of God in our lives.

GOD FORMED COVENANTS with humankind and with the people of Israel so that we might enter into communion with him and share in his friendship. Jesus Christ is the fulfillment of all these covenants, and the Church is the communion of grace in which we, who have been baptized and confirmed in the Holy Spirit, participate in the oneness that is Christ. We are one with him and one with one another. The Eucharist is the consummation of that communion. The New Testament Greek word *koinonia*, which we translate as "communion" or "fellowship," has the sense of *participation*. "The cup of blessing that we bless, is it not a participation (*koinonia*) in the blood of Christ? The bread that we break, is it not a participation (*koinonia*) in the body of Christ?" (1 Cor. 10:16). Jesus Christ is the delight of the saints and the source of their delight and love of one another. Not just our persons but our *relationships* are transformed by his presence.

As human persons, we are fundamentally ordained for relationships: *cor ad cor loquitur*. In this sense, we are fundamentally ecclesial beings—that is, persons who only find their true fulfillment in the Body of Christ, the Church. Your desire for friendship and communion with the Culrosses radiates from your inspired impulse to live his commands as they do. His commands are Truth—and you see the fruits in your five friends. By contrast, you now also see the falsehood of your relationship with Lisa, which you recognize has been based on lust rather than love.

As one of my professors wrote about the human person and community, "Community exists for the sake of friendship and presupposes relationships built on love." The community for which we are destined and for which our heart yearns is the Church, a community of holy men and women brought into union with one another and with Christ, who does not call us servants but friends (John 15:5,13:5). The source and summit of this communion is the Eucharist. The Culrosses are friends of Christ. Their friendship is nourished by the Eucharist, in which their hearts meet his.

The Eucharist creates community and draws all Christian believers—the saints—together in Christ. We are one across time, with all the saints in heaven and the souls of those being purified in purgatory, and across space, with all the baptized around the world. The same divine presence is with us all. In heaven, the saints dwell in a transfigured communion. They have reached the height of personhood. They are without sin—*stabilized in glory*, as Bonaventure says. How do they engage one another and look at one another? What words do they speak? I think they live out the command of St. Dominic: *cum Deo vel de Deo*—to speak only "with God or about God." What would it be like to share in their august company?

I love the saints and have a great affinity for siblings who have become saints. The Culrosses are of this order. The first apostles to be called, Peter and Andrew, were brothers, as were their friends, James and John. St. Benedict (the founder of the Benedictines) and St. Scholastica were twins. They shared a womb together, they shared their faith and the Eucharist, and they were buried in the same tomb. Then there is the amazing family of St. Basil the Great. His parents, St. Basil the Elder and St. Emmelia, were saints; his maternal grandmother St. Macrina the Elder was a saint; his brothers Gregory of Nyssa and Peter of Sebaste were saints, as was his sister, St. Macrina the Younger. That is what my heart desires for all families: that they encounter one another in the Eucharist, which is the most fulfilling communion, a communion with one another in the Trinity.

The Eucharist creates community. Our communities, however, are imperfect. We are not "stabilized by glory." We sin. Our communities, instead of forming us, can instead *deform* us. Seneca, the advisor to Emperor Nero (who burned Rome to the ground and blamed it on the Christians whom he then persecuted) said, "Whenever I have been among men, I come back less a man." He would return from the public square less a man because of the conversations and interactions he shared with sinful people. Do you experience the same deformation, even among your families and friends? When you return from work, are you transformed or deformed by your conversations and by what you witness? When you return from a movie, is your humanity lessened by the images you have seen and that remain in your mind? Where is Christ in your family, among your friends, at work, at the store, in your neighborhood? How does the Eucharist form you to be as Christ in your communities and relationships?

St. Paul, when he wrote letters to the communities he had founded, would often end with a moral exhortation to encourage the disciples along the gospel path. He wrote to the community of believers in Philippi, "Finally, brothers and sisters, whatever is true, whatever is honorable, whatever is just, whatever is pure, whatever is lovely, whatever is gracious, if there is any excellence, and if there is anything worthy of praise, think about these things" (Phil. 4:6-9). The Culrosses help you and one another enter into that communion with Christ, which we find most fully in the Eucharist. The Eucharist creates community, the deepest and fullest human community we can have. John Paul II, in his encyclical on the Church and the Eucharist, quotes a Byzantine scholar who says that in the Eucharist, "unlike any other sacrament, the mystery [of communion] is so perfect that it brings us to the heights of every good thing: here is the ultimate goal of every human desire, because here we attain God and God joins himself to us in the most perfect union."

The Culross family shows you an example of men and women striving to progress along the path of holiness. They give you a glimpse of the communion of saints here on earth. St. Paul expresses the joy of such communion, which I have experienced myself when I visited members of my religious community or the community of family and friends: "For I am longing to see you either to strengthen you by sharing a spiritual gift with you or what is better, to find encouragement among you from our common faith" (Rom. 1:11).

Find encouragement in saints like the Culrosses! Be strengthened! And on this feast of All Saints, look also to the holy men and women in the Church Triumphant. Befriend them. As the Vatican II document on the Church (*Lumen Gentium*) teaches concerning the heavenly saints, "It is most fitting, therefore that we love those friends and co-heirs of Jesus Christ who are also our brothers [and sisters] and outstanding benefactors, and that we give due thanks to God for them."

JOSEPH, I PRAY that you remain in communion with the Culross siblings and form true friendships with them. May your relationships manifest the City of God, which St. Augustine describes in contrast to the City of Man: "The peace of the celestial city is the perfectly ordered and harmonious enjoyment of God, and of one another in God." So often our human friendships and communities are cynical, crude, craven, mocking, inauthentic, mediocre, and prosaic, when they could be genuine, noble, majestic, pure, gracious, honest, and virtuous. St. Francis de Sales wrote about true friendship, "Love everyone with the love of charity, but make friends only with those who can share virtuous love with you. The greater the virtue, the more perfect the friendship. . . . What a blessed privilege to love on earth as we shall love in heaven, and to begin to cherish one another here as we hope to do in eternity!"

Saints like the Culrosses are living stones of the Church whose very persons proclaim the presence of God. With them you sense the nearness of God. They are like the faithful Jews, prophesied about by Zechariah, who fulfill their intercessory role for the nations of the world: "In those days, ten men of nations of every language will take a Jew by the sleeve and say, 'We want to go with you, since we have learned that God is with you'" (Zech. 8:23). Is that not what you felt with these wonderful friends—to be like them, to share in their company, to be formed as they are by the Holy Spirit? How spontaneous the desire to conform your will to theirs. Such is the power and transformation of love—a communion of wills. Such is the union we are to share with God so that our will becomes conformed to his.

You remarked that where you once would have had lustful thoughts about the beauty of women like Marie, Clare, and Aggie, your thoughts and intentions were chaste—or rather, *pure*. Chastity is an external imposition on us when our will is selfishly opposed to the will of God; the purity you experienced with the Culrosses was a conformity of your will to God's will. Be formed by that experience. Take it with you. Be formed by them and become solid in faith and hope and love as they are. I encourage you to take advantage of the invitation to attend Aggie's fencing match next month.

We are ecclesial beings who find our fulfillment in the communion of saints united through Christ, with Christ, and in Christ, in the unity of the Holy Spirit for the glory and honor of the Father. Rejoice in the company of the saints, those in heaven and those here with us. Joseph, be assured of my prayers for you in the communion we share in Christ.

In the eucharistic communion of the saints,

Fr. Terry

PS:

—Go to Mass at least every Sunday.

—Seek friendships and communities that will foster your growth in Christ.

—Draw near to Christ in the Eucharist, and unite your heart to his!

7

To: **Joseph**

Date: **December 4—St. John Damascene**

Re: **FROM PORNOGRAPHY TO ICONOGRAPHY**

Dear Joseph,

Blessed Advent! Since we began the new liturgical year last week I have been pondering your most recent e-mail, which reveals a yearning and struggling for new ways of being and of relating, especially to Aggie Culross, amidst unwanted inclinations and acquiescence to old ways of lust. Joseph, the transition from old to new requires constant attention to who you are and how you will act.

Attention is also the focus of the entire season of Advent, which calls us to "stay awake" and to "keep watch." A favorite Advent image of mine is that of Christians as lookouts on the ship of the Church, which is sailing east toward the arrival of the Lord Jesus Christ in glory at the end of time. With eager anticipation, yet solemn dignity, the lookout arises from his rest and dresses in the darkness. Well-seasoned and disciplined through joy, he feels his way in the dark along corridors and up stairwells, his balanced steps in time with the rise and fall of the ocean waves. Encased in windowless darkness at the end of the final staircase, the lookout grabs the heavy door's handle, turns it, and pushes the door open out onto the deck of the ship and into the cool, fresh night air. It is the breath of the Holy Spirit, which fills his lungs and propels the ship of the Church on her journey.

The lookout climbs the ladder to his observation roost on the main mast, high above the deck. Here he will keep watch in the darkness, awaiting the dawn. All is darkness here, the holy darkness of Advent. Yet it is a darkness not of fear and isolation but of hope and eager anticipation. The darkness is punctuated by stars that draw the human mind and heart into the infinite reaches of the universe, which point to the vastness of the mystery of God: "How rich are the depths of God— how deep his wisdom and knowledge—and how impossible to penetrate his motives or understand his methods" (Rom. 11:33). The stars provide a heavenly companionship on this Advent ocean journey; they give hope and are a sign of providential guidance. They, too, keep tireless watch in joyful obedience: "The glory of the stars makes the beauty of the sky, a brilliant decoration to the heights of the Lord. At the words of the Holy One they stand as he decrees, and never grow slack at their watch" (Sir. 43:9-10). One star—*Stella Maris*—the star of the sea, Our Lady, outshines them all in beauty and humility. Mary is a figure of Advent who embodies in her person Advent hope and joy. She who bore the Incarnate Word, the

Savior of the World, knows in her heart and soul the fulfillment of God's promises to Israel and all of humankind.

The lookout's vigil is not a tiresome struggle for alertness; he is not distracted but is wakeful and alert. All of Creation is yearning: "Who could ever be sated with gazing at his glory?" (Sir. 42:25). The sound of the wind, deep as the sea, carries with it the song of the Church—*Maranatha*, "Come, Lord Jesus." The night of Advent is also pregnant with the message of Christ's Second Coming—the *Parousia*, a Greek word meaning "arrival" or "coming." In Christian terms, *Parousia* is the Second Coming of Christ, which is the consummation of what was begun in the Incarnation and the paschal mystery. It is the definitive manifestation of Christ's glory.

The *Parousia* is our focus during Advent. We are all lookouts awaiting the Lord's coming with eager anticipation. Perhaps today is the Day of the Lord! This hope frames all of our actions and thoughts and words. At the end of each day, at the end of our watch, we retire to our sleeping quarters on the ship of the Church and say, not in dejection but in eager anticipation of the next day, "Today was not the Day of the Lord—perhaps tomorrow. *Maranatha*."

After the Resurrection, the first followers of Jesus—thinking that his return in glory was imminent—prayed, "*Maranatha*. Come, Lord Jesus." Of course, he was with them and is with us always in his Spirit and in the sacraments, especially the Eucharist. Yet, like us they desired his presence without sacramental sign. In the meantime, Christians developed artistic depictions of Jesus to remind them of the One whose return they awaited.

We do the same with our family and friends: we keep pictures or remembrances of them so we can call them to mind
and heart. We long for communion with them in person.
Your e-mail expresses this reality as your thoughts have been
taken up with the Culross family, particularly the women, and
wanting to be in their company. You miss the relationship you
experienced with them, and you yearn for more. You also
note the contrast between the depth of personhood and relationship with Aggie and Clare compared to your relationship
with Lisa, which seemed so focused merely on the physical.
You were wise to break off your relationship with her.

JOSEPH, BE PATIENT with yourself. You are in a state of transformation and transition. I am glad that you encountered the
Culrosses back in October and that you are looking forward
to seeing them again at Aggie's fencing match next week.
This is an advent expectation of sorts in which you are eager
for the arrival of that day to be with them in person. You
mention struggles with purity in thinking about that encounter, but this is a markedly different kind of struggle from what
you experienced when thinking about Lisa. The first days after meeting the Culrosses, you felt a freedom and newness of
being that gave you a sense of who you might become, but by
week's end the old ways and patterns re-emerged. You express
frustration and anger at doing the very things that you don't
want to do. This is exactly the mystery of sin that St. Paul describes in his own life: "What I do, I do not understand. For I

do not do what I want, but I do what I hate" (Rom. 7:15). The path to purity is a long and arduous one that is not traversed in a day or a weekend. Stay awake. Keep watch over yourself.

You felt particularly upset because you brought together the beauty of the Culross women with your habit of lust and selfish sexual expression. Unfulfilled desire for a person, even a desire that begins in purity and in the realm of personhood, can easily sink into the realm of mere bodily desires. Your heart longs for friendship and communion with Aggie, yet you are accustomed to encountering women primarily in a lustful bodily way. You said you feel dirty because even though you weren't thinking of Aggie in a lustful way or wanting to be with her sexually, your longing for her presence was made manifest through selfish sexual stimulation. This connection between desire and body points to the *unity of being* that we are: body and soul. Our mind and body affect one another. Your mind may desire a pure friendship and relationship, but your body can often have a "mind" of its own. You must learn to tame your desires and to govern your body and its responses so that you are truly one and not divided—that you do the things you want to do and avoid that which you don't want to do. Be the lookout keeping watch over your own self.

You also discussed your disgust with your recent return to pornography. The guilt you feel, particularly as you sense how Aggie or Clare would think of you, is a great sign of hope that you are on the right path to freedom. You mentioned that you spent much less time on the websites and that you turned off the computer in disgust. Your attachment to pornography seems to have changed from mere lust for the feminine body to a means for dealing with your loneliness and desire for true communion. These abbreviated computer sessions, to my mind, point to your realization that these images do not satisfy and will never satisfy what your heart yearns for.

DURING THIS ADVENT season we prepare ourselves for the arrival of Christ in glory; of course, we also prepare ourselves to celebrate the Incarnation of the Word: Jesus Christ, fully human and fully divine in one divine Person. In his very humanity, which he shares fully with us except for sin, we encounter God. The man Jesus Christ is the image of God. In the Gospel of St. John, Jesus says, "To have seen me is to have seen the Father" (14:9). St. Paul writes of Jesus, "Seeing the light shed by the good news of the glory of Christ, who is the image of God" (2 Cor. 4:4) and "He is the image of the unseen God" (Col. 1:15). In meeting Jesus Christ, we encounter God. He is the true *icon*, the true image of God; in him, image and reality are one. He is the image, and he *is*.

The early Christians started to depict the image of God, Jesus Christ, in frescoes, icons, paintings, sculpture, and statuary. They even depicted fellow Christians, men and women of faith honored as saints, most particularly the Mother of God, the Blessed Virgin Mary. In the eighth and ninth centuries, however, a great controversy arose in the East concerning these images, which some considered idolatrous. They thought that worship before such images violated the first commandment: "You shall not make yourself a carved image or any likeness of anything in heaven above or on earth beneath or in the waters under the earth; you shall not bow down to them or serve them" (Deut. 5:8). Unlike the idols of carved stone or wood worshipped by the pagans of Old Testament times, the invisible, ineffable God of Israel transcends all materialistic representation. Any depiction of God is not God. But in the mystery of the Incarnation, God becomes visible and tangible in the materiality of human existence. We can see and touch God in Jesus Christ (1 John 1:1).

The Eastern Emperor Leo III declared a war on sacred images in 726 and forbade their use. Iconoclasts—those opposed to the use of sacred images—removed icons and artwork from churches and destroyed them. The saint we celebrate today, John Damascene, was an eighth-century monk of the Eastern Church and Doctor of the Church from Damascus, Syria. He vigorously defended the use of images and their veneration precisely because of the Incarnation. He wrote, "It is clear that when you contemplate God, who is a pure spirit, becoming man for your sake, you will be able to clothe him with the human form. When the Invisible One becomes visible to flesh, you may then draw a likeness of his form. When he who is a pure spirit, without form or limit, immeasurable in the boundlessness of his own nature, existing as God, takes upon himself the form of a servant in substance and in stature, and a body of flesh, then you may draw his likeness, and show it to anyone willing to contemplate it."

The material object of the image is not what we worship. We worship the living God. Damascene, among others, distinguished between different kinds of worship: *adoration* and *veneration.* Adoration (*latria* in Greek) is reserved for the worship given to God alone. Veneration (*dulia*) is the honor given to the saints and angels. Then there is *hyperdulia,* the highest kind of veneration, which we give to the Mother of God. When we use images, we give the proper kind of worship *through* the image, not to it.

Despite the efforts of saints like John Damascene, iconoclasm persisted, and the Second Council of Nicaea met in 787 to resolve the controversy. Nicaea II condemned iconoclasm as heretical and proclaimed the orthodoxy using and worshiping before sacred images. The Council Fathers drew upon the writings of St. John Damascene, among many other Fathers of the Church, in speaking of a "prostration of honor" given to icons: "He who prostrates before the icon does so before the person who is represented therein." On the twelfth centenary of the council, Pope St. John Paul II wrote about the dignity of art and matter as a means to encounter the divine: "Therefore art can represent the form, the effigy of God's human face and lead the one who contemplates it to the ineffable mystery of God made man for our salvation."

A stark contrast exists between this true *icon*ography and pornography. Iconography is a window to heaven that calls forth a true act of worship; through the very matter of the image, the viewer is brought to the reality of the person, divine or human, whose image is depicted. Person meets person in prayerful veneration or adoration. Pornography is not a window to God but a mirror reflecting one's own lustful imagination. Person does not meet person.

Pornography is essentially the Anti-Advent, for the Other never arrives. We remain alone in self-absorption before a lifeless image that cannot satisfy.

In a sense, pornography *is* a type of iconography, but an idolatrous one. Unlike true iconography, which brings about a worship of God, pornography never leaves the realm of this world, because it worships the creature rather than the Creator. Eyes and heart and mind and soul do not look up to the mystery of God but remain locked down on the temporal, material reality before them. The devotee of these pornographic images does not enter into the blessed realm of the Kingdom but sinks into himself and an imaginary world. Pornography obscures and reduces the whole mystery of man and woman to a shadow of corporeality.

What do you notice about yourself when you gaze in such "adoration"? Is it not insatiability? One image is never enough. You become gluttonous, eager for more. You devour the images, which become a part of your world of lust and fantasy; you desire sexual contact; you gaze upon these images not for who the women are but for their bodies and how they can satisfy you. You do not think about whether this woman is a mother with children, about her being someone's daughter or sister, or about her friendships. Pornography is self-directed; it does not orient you outward, only inward. Pornography is not only idolatrous worship, but it is also self-worship. You seek to satisfy only your own desires. You become the only person in your own imaginary world. Pornographic icons isolate. They lead you only to yourself.

Time hurls past as more and more images are sought and "venerated." You become a slave to the senses, as with that depicted in Proverbs: "I have made my bed gay with quilts, spread the best Egyptian sheets; I have sprinkled my bed with myrrh, with aloes and with cinnamon. Come, let us drink deep of love until the morning, and abandon ourselves to delight. Bemused he follows her like an ox being led to the slaughter, like a stag caught in a noose, till he is pierced to the liver by an arrow, like a bird darting into a snare not knowing its life is at stake" (7:16-18).

These images not only anti-icons of God; they also reveal a false femininity and humanity. Unlike their wise virgin counterparts in iconography, the women depicted in pornography do not know the dignity of their being, nor the splendor of their Creator. Their posture, gestures, and eyes point to an urgent temporality, confining man's purpose to this world and this moment. Instead of pointing beyond the image, they draw the viewer into it as an end unto itself. They are women without boundaries; their beings are porous; they know not what they do as they expose the treasure of their beings to the eager eyes and hands of pirates intent on stealing it. They despoil themselves like pearls before swine.

The idolatry of pornographic veneration denies both death and any awareness of the eternal realm of God, luring you into a false world of eternal youth. Iconography is a window to the eternal realm of God where there is life everlasting with God; pornography is a trap door sinking into a temporal stasis that spurns the creation of time for a Never-Never Land of sexual escapism. As Hugh Hefner, the founder of *Playboy,* put it, "It's Peter Pan time. I'm living a grown-up version of a boy's dream."

Rejecting the reality of time, pornography is not only the Anti-Advent but the Anti-*Parousia*. It spurns the vigilant journey toward the fulfillment of our world and of our persons in favor of an eternal adolescence of stunted humanity.

Joseph, you must move from pornography to iconography. You must move from idolatrous worship of pornographic icons to the true worship of God and veneration of the saints.

St. Gregory of Nyssa differentiates between the pure man and the *profligate* man. He says that we see the difference in what is valued in each man's house: "In the house of the one there are frescoes on the wall which by their artful pictures inflame the sensual passions. These things bring out the nature of the illness, and through the eye passion pours in upon the soul from the dishonorable things which are seen. But in the house of the prudent man there is every precaution and foresight to keep the eye pure from sensual spectacles."

Be the lookout and fill your heart and mind and eyes with holy images, with true icons, and purify yourself of all unholy icons. Do not bring "sensual spectacles" into the sanctuary of your heart and mind. Gaze upon holy images of Jesus Christ, of Mary, the saints, and angels. Foster a love and devotion of sacred art and prostrate your heart and being before the reality signified in the iconography. Encounter the fullness of the mystery of the human person through your reverence of iconographic presentations. Jesus Christ is the true Icon of God. St. John Damascene said that "Church art must aim at speaking the language of the Incarnation and, with the elements of matter express the One who 'deigned to dwell in matter and bring about our salvation through matter.'" Venerating true icons will drive from your heart not only the false idol of pornography but other idols of our trivial and materialistic culture: sports, movies, electronic toys. As John Paul II wrote, it will help us combat "the depersonalizing and at times degrading effects of the many images that condition our lives in advertisements and the media, for [the icon is] an image that turns toward us the look of Another invisible one and gives us access to the reality of the eschatological world." Elsewhere he notes how sacred art "molds" matter in a way that leads us to adoration. Pornography, in contrast, molds matter in a way that leads us away from the mystery of God and toward adoration of the flesh.

Human imagination, ingenuity, and craftsmanship—all gifts of our humanity from God—can create artistic works of beauty that lead us into the divine and to adoration of the mystery. Church architecture itself can lift the human spirit to transcendent heights; sacred art of windows, mosaics, statues, and sculpture can do the same. But greater still is God's artwork of Creation, especially his masterpiece the human person. *We* are living images—icons—of God. The human icon—the *imago Dei*—is the most beautiful of all, for it is matter molded by God and infused with the breath of his Spirit.

Joseph, move from pornography to iconography. The more you deepen your friendships with living icons, such as Aggie, the more easily you will reject pornographic icons. When we arrive at the truth, we want to remain there.

In this season of Advent, as we await the arrival of Christ, be the lookout and look to that brightest star in the sky, *Stella Maris*, Mary, the Mother of God. Venerate her image with *hyperdulia* and draw close to her who is blessed among all women. As Dante describes Mary in heaven, she has a "beauty that was joy in the eyes of all the other saints."

Know of my prayers for you during this time of joyful anticipation, especially in the Eucharist.

In the joy of Christ, the Icon of God,

Fr. Terry

PS:

—Make an effort every day to let your eyes see only holy images.

—Practice seeing the people around you as icons of God.

—Stay awake and watchful!

8

To: **Joseph**

Date: **January 17—St. Antony of the Desert**

Re: **RE-WORDING YOUR LIFE**

Dear Joseph,

May God's word be in your thoughts and on your lips and in your heart! The words of your e-mail struck me. You described how simply seeing a billboard advertisement for an "adult" bookstore can initiate a chain of thoughts that captures your attention and leads you down a path that has all too familiar results. You described similar reactions to a magazine cover at the checkout counter, with its sensuous female model and the headlines promising new ways to please one's partner. Even an innocuous search on the internet all too often results in unwanted links to sexually explicit ads.

The power of just a single word can change our lives. The billboard, the magazine cover, the internet ads—all of these either include or allude to the word "sex." That one word can capture a man's thoughts.

Contrast that word and those thoughts with the words you

exchanged with Aggie on the phone and in e-mails and texts, and how they raised your thoughts to the level of the person and encouraged you to respond nobly to her.

Joseph, a direct relationship exists between our words and our thoughts. Language is central to our identity. We are born into a world of language, which is essential for our full development as a person, and this development takes place communally. We listen to others. We learn from their words. We trust their words. We are fed with words. Words shape and form us. They can lift our hearts and move us to be someone better. Words form our thoughts, and they form our life. Without words our humanity is diminished, but worse, the wrong words deform us.

What words do we listen to? (That is, what thoughts of others do we listen to?) What words do we say in our minds? What do we think throughout the day? Whom do we become through words, through thoughts, and through actions based on those words and thoughts?

If you took the effort to tabulate how much time you spend thinking about a given topic, what words would you find represented the most? Sleep, food, work, bills, family, friends, sports, entertainment, exercise, sex, the past, the future, God? What words are absent that should be present? What *could* you be thinking about instead?

Joseph, if you truly want to be free of lust and worldliness—free of pornography, fantasies, vain interests, and selfish pleasures—you must change your thoughts and your words. *Re-word your life!*

Re-wording your life is learning a whole new language. As with any language, it is part of a culture. So, this re-wording, this new language, requires a completely new culture and community. St. Augustine wrote about two communities and cultures, the City of Man and the City of God. These are two ways of living, two cultural, linguistic modes of being among a community. The City of Man is a selfish culture of vice with a corresponding vocabulary of words and thoughts. The City of God is a community of men and women formed by the Word of God. The City of God requires the language of the Word of God. You've certainly been introduced to that city by your participation in the friendship and communion with Aggie and her family and friends.

The City of Man operates with an anthropological vision of man as driven only to fulfill his own desires—to obey his thirst, as the old soft drink commercial said. Such language distorts us; it throws us out of equilibrium. Instead of our intellect and mind making prudent decisions about when, what, and how much to drink, the mind is the slave of the body's impulses. Instead of recognizing sexual love's place in the context of marriage, our culture encourages the fulfillment of sexual desires without the limits of any context. Books, magazines, and websites proclaim the good news about sexual relationships outside of marriage and describe in detail how to improve sexual technique for maximum pleasure. They preach words of sexual fulfillment, satisfaction, and body parts.

Absent in this language of sexual pleasure are words about

the truth of the human person, the truth about love, the truth about procreation, the truth about marriage, the truth about virginity. Exploration, experimentation, satisfaction of desires, and fulfillment of pleasure—these are the measures of our sexuality for the culture of the City of Man, which worships the Word of Lust.

Are you ready instead to be formed by the Word of God, to do whatever he tells you, as Mary told the servants at the wedding feast of Cana (John 2:5)? Re-wording your life requires a firmness of purpose and discipline, the discipline of an athlete or musician or doctor. To become a Man of God requires first God's grace but then our response—to think about holiness, to think about truth and goodness and beauty, to think about God, and to fill our mind with words that are true, that correspond to the Word of God himself.

St. Paul writes about the seriousness of purpose, the discipline required to live this life in Christ:

> Do you not know that the runners in the stadium all run in the race, but only one wins the prize? Run so as to win. Every athlete exercises discipline in every way. They do it to win a perishable crown, but we an imperishable one. Thus I do not run aimlessly; I do not fight as if I were shadowboxing. No, I drive my body and train it, for fear that, after having preached to others, I myself should be disqualified (1 Cor. 9:24-27).

Do you live with this purpose, or do you shadowbox through life, without awareness of who you can be? When you encounter God, do you want to hold nothing back? Do you want to give him your all?

TODAY WE CELEBRATE the memorial of St. Antony of the Desert. He lived in Egypt in the third and fourth centuries and is one of the founders of monasticism. When he was about twenty, he sold all he had and ventured out to live alone in the tombs outside the city; at thirty-five he went out into the desert of Egypt, where he remained for the next seventy years of his life. For the most part, he lived alone. From his first waking to falling asleep, what words did he think about in his solitude? What discipline was required to train his thoughts on what is good and holy and to banish what is evil?

St. Athanasius, who had met St. Antony and subsequently wrote a biography about him, gives us a glimpse of Antony's thoughts:

> For all the monks who came to him he unfailingly had the same message: to have faith in the Lord and love him; to guard themselves from lewd thoughts and pleasures of the flesh; to flee vanity, and to pray constantly; to sing holy songs before sleep and after, and to take heart the precepts in Scripture; to keep in mind the deeds of the saints, so that the soul, ever mindful of the commandments, might be educated by their ardor.

The culture of the Church formed Antony. He was nourished by the Word of God in Scripture. He meditated upon
the lives of the saints as living words.

These thoughts required discipline and asceticism. In the
early years of his desert solitude, Antony was afflicted with
violent temptations of the flesh, but he conquered the devil through prayer, fasting, self-knowledge, and, foremost, the
grace of God:

> [The devil] advanced against the youth, noisily disturbing
> him by night, and so troubling him in the daytime that even
> those who watched were aware of the bout that occupied
> them both. The one hurled foul thoughts and the other
> overturned them through his prayers; the former resorted
> to titillation, but the latter, seeming to blush, fortified the
> body with faith and with prayers and with fasting. And
> the beleaguered devil undertook one night to assume the
> form of a woman and to imitate her every gesture, solely in
> order that he might beguile Antony. But in thinking about
> Christ and considering the excellence won through him . . .
> Antony extinguished the fire of his opponent's deception.

The pathway to purity is arduous and never free of temptation. Yet, as you progress along that path, your exercise of
virtue increases and you will more readily choose the good
with quickness, ease, and joy. As St. Paul tells us, "We are those
who have the mind of Christ" (1 Cor. 2:16). You must think
his thoughts. To think the thoughts of Christ, you must desire
them. You must have a firm purpose. Antony teaches us that

we can start by interiorizing the very word *virtue* itself. It is a word that forms our thoughts and our character, as Athanasius exhorts: "Do not be afraid to hear about virtue, and do not be a stranger to the term. For it is not distant from us, nor does it stand external to us, but its realization lies in us, and the task is easy if only we shall will it." The way of virtue, says Athanasius, is "measured by the aspirant's desire and purposefulness." Do you *will* to change?

The devil despised "seeing such purpose in a youth" as Antony. Unable to defeat him by confronting him directly with temptations of the flesh, Athanasius writes, the devil sought to fill Antony with thoughts that would distract him from his purpose: "So he raised in his mind a great dust cloud of considerations, since he wished to cordon him off from his righteous intention." The devil suggested to Antony "memories of his possessions, his guardianship of his sister, the bonds of kinship, love of money and of glory, the manifold pleasure of food, the relaxations of life, and finally, the rigor of virtue, and how great the labor is that earns it, suggesting also the bodily weakness and the length of time involved."

What words and memories and pleasures fill your mind each moment? Are you aware of them? How do you respond to them? Do you recognize those thoughts that are dangerous to your soul? Do you readily dismiss them as temptations that lead you away from God? Do you discipline your intellect to think of what is holy and virtuous?

Antony's central purpose was a desire to know and love God. He was inspired by hearing the Gospel passages of Matthew: "If you would be perfect, go, sell what you possess and give it to the poor, and you will have treasure in heaven" and "Do not be anxious about tomorrow" (Matt. 5:48; 6:34). He headed out into the desert to be one with God. Part of his firm purpose was "to present himself as the sort of person ready to appear before God—that is, pure of heart and prepared to obey his will, and no other." He would be formed by the Word of God, to follow his commandments, and Mary's— "Do whatever he tells you."

Antony disciplined his mind and his body through prayer and fasting and the effort of his will. This grace-filled discipline distinguished Antony from his peers. He lived to be 105, a specimen of physical and spiritual virtue. "He was one of God's athletes," Athanasius describes him in his biography. "It was not his physical dimensions that distinguished him from the rest, but the stability of character and the purity of the soul. His soul being free of confusion, he held his outer senses also undisturbed, so that from the soul's joy his face was cheerful as well, and from the movements of the body it was possible to sense and perceive the stable condition of the soul."

One of the concrete ways Antony developed this stability of character was by practicing an awareness of and responsiveness to his own thoughts as if they were evident to other people. For although our actions may sometimes indirectly reveal them, for the most part our thoughts lie hidden, and this can be dangerous. As with our actions, we would be less likely to sin if our thoughts were observable to others. Would you not act differently if you knew you had to give a report to Aggie of what you explored on the internet? Would you not discipline your thoughts more carefully if other people could read the words inside your head? That is the very practice Antony used, as described by St. Athanasius:

> Let each of us note and record our actions and the stirrings of our souls as though we were going to give an account to each other. And you can be sure that, being particularly ashamed to have them made known, we would stop sinning and even meditating on something evil. For who wants to be seen sinning? Or who, after sinning, would not prefer to lie, wanting it to remain unknown? So then, just as we would not practice fornication if we were observing each other directly, so also we will doubtless keep ourselves from impure thoughts, ashamed to have them known, if we record our thoughts as if reporting them to each other.

OUR LIVES ARE not isolated and individual, because we are *communal* and *ecclesial* beings. The Christian is never an autonomous person separated from the Body of Christ. Such isolation is the pride of life wherein one wants to be one's own god. Should not our lives be transparent displays of who we are? What attracts us to holy people is that very oneness of purpose and transparency; they are men and women who have wrestled with themselves and emerged victorious through self-denial, humility, discipline, and prayer. Interior and exterior are one.

Part of the initial difficulty in conversion from the language and culture of lust to the language and culture of virtue is a disequilibrium within your being. How far from equilibrium are you? Will you be divided against yourself, or will you move toward peace with your own body? In this transition, your intellect and will are directed to a new good—virtue—but you are disturbed because you have not yet integrated your bodily passions into this new way of being. You approach serenity and equilibrium when through discipline you quiet your passions, allowing your intellect and will to respond more freely and easily to reason and grace. At equilibrium, where body and soul are in just relation, you are like the "king enthroned on a judgment seat; with one look [he] scatters all that is evil" (Prov. 20:8).

Athanasius described Antony as one who "maintained utter equilibrium . . . The state of his soul was one of purity, for it was not constrained by grief, nor relaxed by pleasure." Antony, who had reached this level of equilibrium through disciplining his mind and body, readily dismissed temptation and evil thoughts. In similar fashion, St. Augustine described the man who dwells in the City of God as one who has a "serene avoidance of sin" and whose "body [is] under the bidding of the will." Joseph, in order to achieve that serenity and equilibrium, you must have the mind of Christ; your mind must be filled and formed by the Word of God. A mind fascinated with the Word of Lust disturbs the body instead of bringing it peace. A direct relationship exists between serene holiness and the time the mind is occupied with thoughts of God. Augustine added that "the less the soul has God in mind in all its thinking, the less it is subordinated to God; and the more the desires of the flesh oppose the spirit, the less subordinate is the body to the soul."

Antony confronted himself in the desert solitude. Free of distractions, he had only himself and his thoughts and will to contend with. We who live in the world must also confront ourselves in the desert if we are to re-word our lives. In the desert, we strip ourselves of the culture of the world and enter the culture of God's kingdom, where, free of man's creations and stimulations, we can listen more attentively to his Word. As the prophet Hosea proclaimed to the people of Israel, "That is why I am going to lure her and lead her out into the wilderness and speak to her heart" (Hos. 2:16).

The desert is that place where we encounter stillness and silence and can be alone with God. Joseph, you may withdraw to that desert simply by going to your room and turning off all of your electronic devices. Spend time daily removed from artificial stimuli—all those technological creations of humankind. You may enter the desert by taking a walk in the woods or a park, without headphones, with ears open to hear the sounds or words of God's creation. In solitude, silence, and stillness, listen, watch, and wait. In your active passivity, you attend to God's activity. As you enter the wilderness, you enter God's creation, with its own rhythms and pace. You are a guest in a mystery that precedes you. You encounter God's creation, ancient and subtle.

The desert helps you listen to the Word of God free from the distractions of the world, free from words that deform rather than form you. In the silence and solitude and stillness, you are able to listen to your heart. Instead of merely reacting to stimuli and suggested thoughts, you have the time and silence to choose what you will think about—to manage and control the words that direct your life.

Go to the desert and confront yourself each day. Think about your choice of words and thoughts. How many words do you speak in a day? How many are necessary? How many are virtuous? How many words do you read or hear each day—texts, telephone conversations, television, songs, internet, e-mails, videos? What shall you do with your time? What words shall you listen to? What words shall you read? Each moment, you form or deform yourself based on what you think and do and say.

To re-word your life also demands a zealous attention to *time*. Romano Guardini was a theologian of the twentieth century who wrote,

> Being genuinely good would mean that we would accomplish in every hour what that hour required, and thus life would ascend to the fullness of its achievement and perfection as called for by God. What is not done now cannot, however, be made good later on, because every hour comes but once, and the next has, once again, its own demands. What becomes of the gaps and voids in this continually passing life? And how do things stand with what has been done wrongly? . . . What has been done rests in being. What will become of that when time has run out and man can do nothing more?

Joseph, the great wrestling match with yourself lies before you. Holiness comes not from a general life but an attention to each moment. How do you form yourself each hour, each moment, by the Word of God?

Be assured of my prayers for you, especially in the Eucharist.

In the living Word of God,

Fr. Terry

PS:

—Practice being aware of your thoughts as if others could hear them.

—Spend time each day in silence and solitude, letting God speak to you.

—Re-word your life with the Word of God!

9

To: **Joseph**

Date: **February 10—St. Scholastica**

Re: **FRIENDSHIP**

Dear Joseph,

I was crossing campus last week and found myself on a collision course with a man and a woman approaching one another from opposite directions. I slowed down to let the woman pass in front of me as she headed toward her friend. Her face was bright with a wonderful smile. I thought to myself, "Is that how I go to meet God in prayer?" Do we go to God with smiles on our faces and with hearts lifted up, as we do when we are going to a friend's house? Are we filled with thanksgiving at this gift of friendship? Let us give him thanks for what he has accomplished in his plan of salvation through Jesus Christ in the Holy Spirit.

Have you ever reflected on the joy of friendship? As a priest I have been particularly inspired by the tender and holy friendships between priests/brothers and religious sisters. For example, I delight in the friendship between the thirteenth-century Dominicans, Bl. Jordan and Bl. Diana. Jordan succeeded St. Dominic as the master-general of the Dominicans, and his letters to Diana, one of the three original Dominican nuns, still exist. "Whatever you may lack of my presence which you cannot have," he wrote to her, "gain from the presence of a better friend, your spouse Jesus Christ. . . He is our bond by which my spirit is linked to yours."

As Christians, all of our relationships, too, should be anchored in Christ and accompanied by him. St. Aelred of Rievaulx, twelfth-century English Cistercian monk and abbot, began his medieval treatise on spiritual friendship with the words, "Here we are, you and I, and I hope a third, Christ, is in our midst." Joseph, all that we do should be done in Christ, and that most wonderfully includes our friendships. Your latest e-mail suggests that you are developing such a friendship with Aggie.

You describe this new friendship as unlike any other you have ever had. You have finally met a woman who takes seriously her life of faith in Jesus Christ, and it unsettles you. Yes, indeed, the first encounter with a person who speaks about Jesus as someone vitally and vibrantly present, who speaks openly about faith and even, as you note, virginity for the sake of Jesus, can be jarring.

I smiled when I read that you had never prayed with someone over the phone before Aggie ended your first phone call by asking if you wanted to pray. For those who are not used to prayer outside of liturgical settings, the experience of praying with friends can be awkward at first. It calls forth a new, intimate way of relating to those friends and to God.

You have had many Catholic friends and classmates, but none of them speak so forthrightly about Jesus as Aggie does. For her, faith is not some vague backdrop to life, taken for granted but ultimately irrelevant. When she prays to God, she is speaking to someone real and present in the room. She takes seriously Jesus' promise, "I will be with you always until the end of time" (Matt. 28:20).

The saints, of course, are glorious examples of others who enjoyed an intimate friendship with Christ. The martyrs spilled their blood not for an idea but for a Person whom they loved and worshiped. Even where Christians were not killed in "red" martyrdom, others, to show the depth of their love for Jesus, practiced "white" martyrdom through lives of asceticism. They went into the desert as hermits and monks; they took vows of celibacy and virginity. As monasticism began to grow, these men and women saw themselves as the successors to the martyrs. The white martyrs died for Christ by devoting every moment of their lives to him. Rather than suffering one stroke of the sword, the white martyrs contended with a thousand pin pricks.

Whether red or white, all forms of martyrdom have the same fundamental basis, summarized by St. Benedict in his Rule: "To put nothing before the love of Christ."

I think that Aggie is one of those women who puts nothing before the love of Christ. Friendship with her then necessarily involves admitting him into your relationship. You have described how different your conversations are with her than with your other female friends. What struck me was that not only has the content of your conversations changed but the context of the content has been re-shaped or re-formed. With Aggie, talk about plans for the future shifts from being a *career* and something you make on your own to being a *vocation*. Christ's call enters into the discussion where previously he was absent. God's Providence is a new context in which you see and evaluate your life and then discuss it with Aggie, from the vast arc of your life into the future to the day to day moments and decisions. Though she is a collegiate athlete, sports is not an idle topic as an end in itself. It is subordinated to the person and ethics and social concerns. What may be presumed, ignored, or rejected in previous friendships about the world and the human person is made explicit in your relationship with Aggie: the world is freely created by God, and humans are made in God's image. In contrast to a secular ideology and anthropology, she thinks with the mind of Christ and the Church, and you are developing that vision and vocabulary as well. The basis for your friendship with one another is God's call for all people to share in his friendship.

JESUS TELLS HIS disciples in his farewell discourse at the Last Supper, "I no longer call you servants but friends" (John 15:15). We are his friends if we keep his commandments. Friends share a common view and way of life. Friendship with Jesus not only entails living a life in accord with who Jesus is and what he taught, but it also necessarily includes friendship with the friends of Jesus—the Church. Friendship with fellow Christians necessarily includes a mutual friendship with

Jesus Christ in the Holy Spirit. Friendship with Aggie necessarily involves friendship with Jesus Christ, and friendship with Christ always demands a life of continual conversion. Don't you see this truth already at work in your life?

You acknowledge that Aggie has given you a new perspective on women. Your former friendships with women, particularly your relationship with Lisa, focused primarily on the physical. Your relationships with women during college consisted of hanging out with them, working on group projects, and an occasional beer-induced making out at a party. You might have gone to Mass with them on Sunday, but you never discussed your faith. Mass was mainly a social event.

Your male friends were mostly Catholic, but their faith was superficial at best. You have mentioned their frequent attempts to sleep with someone they found at a party. Sunday mornings were times to hear about the events of the weekend, which usually involved copious amounts of alcohol and sexual encounters with women they barely knew. Conversation about women was often coarse and sexual. If anyone mentioned virginity, it was in the context of leaving it behind. Some of the guys regarded a young woman's virginity as a burden; for others it was an added allure motivating them to pursue her more aggressively.

Your conversations with Aggie stand in stark contrast to that coarse, boozy milieu. Consider the unicorn picture she texted you from her trip to Rome the previous summer. As you know, the unicorn is part of a golden carving on the wall near the main entrance to St. Peter's Basilica. It depicts the head and front leg of a unicorn, whose horn is held by the hand of a woman. Although it may seem strange to include a mythical animal within this church built atop the burial place of St. Peter, the unicorn is a symbol both of the Incarnation and of purity and virginity. In mythology, a unicorn sought out purity and would seek to lay its head on the lap of a pure virgin. With Mary as the Virgin, the unicorn is associated then with Christ and his Incarnation.

You expressed surprise that a woman, a senior in college, could speak so overtly about a life of virginity, yet you found her attitude not prudish but somehow attractively *feminine*. That's because her virginity is not simply a decision against sexual activity but is intimately tied to her relationship with Jesus. She is chaste because of and for him. He rules her heart and her friendships. Like her sister Clare, she has chosen virginity not out of fear but out of love. Clare hopes to profess the vow of celibacy as a sister, and Aggie desires to be a virgin until she marries. "To put nothing before the love of Christ." Aggie told you that the witness of the virgins throughout the history of the Church—women such as Lucy and Cecilia, Agnes and Clare, Gertrude and Catherine of Siena, and Kateri Tekakwitha and Thérèse of Lisieux—inspired and formed her sister and her.

Our environment forms us. Aggie and Clare grew up with a conscience formed by their family and friends, including the saints. It is a delight to speak with others about a mutual desire for holiness and to encourage one another in that effort. Cardinal Ratzinger wrote that being a Christian calls for *fellowship*. "God," he said, "comes to a human being only through other human beings. Even in the realm of the spirit the human person is an unfinished being; even in the realm of spirit the principle holds that we can exist as human beings only with the help of one another and for one another."

Aggie's presence is unique in your life. You have never had a close, adult friendship with a woman who is a virgin. The women you knew best in college were either girlfriends of the guys in the dorm—and there was no secret that most of them were sleeping together—or your other female friends who had boyfriends with whom they were sexually active.

Joseph, it seems that Aggie is calling you to be like the unicorn who seeks out purity rather than lust. Friendship with Aggie requires a new way of relating to women and a new way of relating, period. This friendship necessarily involves a third person—Jesus Christ. It demands a purity of heart. It demands a mutual friendship in Christ. It demands that you "put nothing before the love of Christ." Christian friendship—friendship in Christ—is a relationship lived deliberately in the Kingdom.

TRUE FRIENDSHIP IS not merely about shared activities or interests, or simple camaraderie. Aristotle identified three types of friendship—friendship based on utility, pleasure, and good people. He concluded that, unlike relationships based on utility or pleasure, "Complete friendship is the friendship of good people similar in virtue." St. Aelred of Rievaulx, over a millennium later, echoed that distinction: "Hence let one kind of friendship be called carnal, another worldly, and another spiritual. The carnal springs from mutual harmony in vice; the worldly is enkindled by the hope of gain; and the spiritual is cemented by similarity of life, morals, and pursuits among the just."

Today, we celebrate the memorial of St. Scholastica, the twin sister of St. Benedict, the sixth-century monk and founder of the Benedictines. Their friendship was begun as siblings but transformed and elevated by being brother and sister in Christ. They shared a womb and a tomb. More importantly, as "white martyrs" they shared friendship with Jesus Christ. St. Scholastica dedicated herself to God from an early age and founded a monastery of nuns near St. Benedict's monastery at Monte Cassino. Scholastica and Benedict would meet once a year at a small building near Mount Cassino and spend a day in spiritual dialogue.

Their last meeting exemplifies their love and friendship in Christ. After receiving a premonition that her death was near, Scholastica implored her brother to stay past his regular hour for departure so that they could continue their spiritual conversation. Benedict insisted that obedience to his Rule demanded his return. Undaunted, Scholastica bowed her head in prayer. Just then, a powerful thunderstorm broke out, preventing Benedict and his companions from leaving. He looked accusingly at his sister and asked, "What have you done?"

Brother and sister then spoke untiringly throughout the entire night about heavenly delights. Benedict finally parted from Scholastica in the morning and returned to the monastery. Three days later, from his cell window, he saw Scholastica's soul in the form of a dove rising up to heaven. He buried her body in the tomb he had prepared for himself. His body was buried beside hers four years later.

Benedict and Scholastica are models of Christian love and friendship. Their holy encounter of one another in Christ reveals the basis for a friendship between any Christian man and woman. Their conversation was pure and free from vulgar expressions or thoughts. They delighted in one another from a true concern for the other's fulfillment. They desired the same noble perfection in Christ, to live a life filled with the Holy Spirit. They exemplified what Aelred wrote: "And so in friendship are joined honor and charm, truth and joy, sweetness and good-will, affection and action. And all these take their beginning from Christ, advance through Christ, and are perfected in Christ."

Ask Benedict and Scholastica to pray for you so that your friendship with Aggie, having begun in Christ, may advance though him and be perfected in him. Cicero wrote that friendship is "mutual harmony… coupled with benevolence and charity." Christian friendship is indeed a mutual harmony, a sharing of hearts within a bond of trust and love, but it goes beyond mutual sharing to include a friendship with Jesus Christ. True friends reverence one another in and with him. As you and Aggie grow in friendship, walk together with Jesus along its path. Seek, as Aelred advised in the early stages of friendship, "purity of intention, the direction of reason, and restraint of moderation."

Friendship is a great gift. Scripture speaks of its goodness for humankind: "Fragrant oil gladdens the heart, friendship's sweetness comforts the soul" (Prov. 27:9). Joseph, you are in my prayers as you enter into this friendship with Aggie. May the friendship be pure and true, for friendship is of God. As Aelred, adapting St. John's truth that God is love, wrote, "God is friendship . . . and he that abides in friendship, abides in God, and God in him."

Know of my prayer for you in the Eucharist.

In Christ's friendship,

Fr. Terry

PS:

    —Choose friends who think and speak about noble topics.

    —Don't be afraid to pray with friends and talk about Jesus with them.

    —Be friends with Christ!

10

To: **Joseph**

Date: **March 19—St. Joseph**

Re: **COHABITATION**

Dear Joseph,

S ilence and solitude surround me in the dimly illuminated
crypt church of St. Joseph's Oratory in Montreal. I offered
Mass for you on this, your patronal feast. The silence amidst
the vaulted arches and wooden pews has a fullness and purpose, like the silence of St. Joseph.

In all of the New Testament, Joseph speaks no words. He is
silent, but his silence is not a mark of absence. Joseph's silence
reveals his strength as a righteous man of God, responsive
to God's will and the plan of salvation in Jesus Christ. It is
not the silence of one painfully shy or socially awkward; it is
the silence of one who ponders great mysteries, of one who
accepts great responsibility and does not squander breath on
trivialities. His is the silence of a man bound to God, listening
and attentive to God's Word.

Joseph stands in that long line of men holy before God and

peers. Noah, Moses, Caleb, Joshua, Elijah, Jonah, and Joseph—
these were men of God. Their relationships with God defined
their identities. Their gravity demonstrates their steadfast and
purposeful character. We cannot think of these men apart
from their receptivity to God's will and their participation in
God's plan of salvation, and these forty days of Lent can help
us in our struggle to become one of them.

Elijah walked for forty days and nights to Mt. Horeb and
encountered God, not in the mighty wind, or earthquake,
or fire, but in a still small voice (1 Kings 9:11-12). Silence
and stillness enabled Elijah to hear God. Joseph's silence was
potent and effective because it enabled him also to hear and
respond decisively to the divine call to be Mary's husband
and the legal father of Jesus. Joseph's silence heralded the way
of God; it revealed his God-centeredness. Where are the men
of God today? Men seem most noticeable by their absence.
Instead of the silence of Joseph, modern men so often participate in and contribute to the noise of self-absorption and
self-gratification. So many men do not listen for the Word of
God. They are attracted to the worldly sounds around them.
Joseph, you touched on this reality of modern masculinity in
your description of your recent visit with your former college
friend and his girlfriend at their apartment. I admire your
steadfastness of faith in finding a Mass on Sunday morning
even though your friends, who were raised Catholic, chose
not to accompany you. I agree that something seems to be
missing in their relationship, even though they do everything
a married couple would do.

What is missing in cohabiting couples is precisely a profession of vows to one another before a community and before God. They are attracted to the noise of the world, participate in it, and allow themselves and their cacophonous activity to drown out the still, small voice of matrimony. Critical words remain unspoken—words that create the foundation on which to build a lifetime together. They are a couple without commitment. Without the marriage vows, they are also lacking righteousness.

THE GOSPEL OF Matthew describes Joseph as a "righteous" man. That is a word we do not often hear in our culture. It sounds so . . . well, self-righteous. But righteousness is simply a life directed wholly to God. Righteousness is subjection to and acceptance of the whole of God's will.

Isn't the absence of vows between a man and woman who live together an absence of righteousness? There is a sharp contrast between the modern man who cohabits with a woman and Joseph, who, though betrothed to Mary, did not live with her.

In first-century Judaism, the betrothal rite legally joined a young man and woman together, though the woman remained at the house of her father. During the betrothal, the man would visit his bride regularly. By the time of the marriage ceremony, which sanctioned marital relations, the couple had gotten to know each other in a respectful manner under the supervision of their families. On the other hand, many modern cohabiting couples take the opposite approach, engaging in sexual activity almost immediately after meeting and only later getting to know each other and their families.

Joseph's relationship with Mary flows from his relationship with God. His life stands as a model for how a man should relate to and care for a woman, particularly during their dating and engagement. In his righteousness, when Joseph discovered Mary's pregnancy, he decided to divorce her quietly, rather than initiate official proceedings that would expose her to shame.

In his righteousness, Joseph followed the law in joining with Mary to present Jesus in the temple forty days after his birth. In his righteousness, he responded to God's message in a dream by fleeing to Egypt with Mary and Jesus to protect his foster son from Herod's murderous intentions.

Everything Joseph did was in relationship with God's will. By his deeds, he bore silent witness to a life of holiness and humility before God. He was a man of prayer and a deep interior life that allowed him to hear, identify, and respond to the voice of God calling him to this vocation of guardianship and fatherhood. He heard the Word of God, who shepherds his people and calls them to himself.

Joseph's foster son Jesus identified himself as the Good Shepherd who has come to seek the lost sheep and draw all to himself. Years ago, I heard this story from a Dominican priest about a Jordanian Catholic shepherd:

East of the Jordan River in the land of Jordan was a small, poor Catholic parish. One morning a, shepherd awoke to find half of his flock of two dozen sheep stolen. Angry, sad, and distraught, he sought out the parish priest not only for consolation but also because he was the only one with a car. So the priest and shepherd set out to look for the sheep. They made their way to the town center and the market where abundant goods are sold every day. They sought out the market master who oversees the buying and selling. He took them to the sheep pen, an enclosed area with hundreds of sheep and livestock.

The shepherd looked at all the sheep and wondered if he would ever find his sheep, and if so how would he prove that they were his. In a loud voice, he cried out over the sounds of trading in the market, calling for his sheep. In amongst the sheep he could see movement. He continued to call out in his voice, and he saw sheep moving toward him. He continued to call, and soon there before him were his twelve sheep. Some of the sheep in the pen never heard the sound of the voice; it was indistinguishable from all the background noise. Others heard the voice but did not recognize it. Only these twelve recognized the voice of their shepherd, the one who fed them every day, who called them in from the pasture, the one who cared and tended them, the one who protected them from wild animals and other dangers. They recognized his voice.

Many of today's men do not seem to recognize the voice of Jesus Christ the Good Shepherd, calling to them amidst the noise of the world that drowns out and contradicts his voice. Too often, both men and women are unrighteous, ignoring the will of God as they follow the way of the world and their own will. It can be hard to find the righteous men who wait until marriage to live with their betrothed, thereby honoring the dignity of both parties and the sacrament of marriage.

Cohabiting engaged couples preparing for marriage claim to want the Church, yet by their actions, they also reject the Church. They (or perhaps their parents) want a beautiful and meaningful wedding in a Catholic setting rather than a brief, impersonal civil ceremony. They recognize that God and the Church are important, yet they also reject what God and the Church demand of them. Indeed, nearly every cohabiting couple I have counseled about marriage declare that they consider themselves already married. If they are already married—living together and doing everything married couples do (except, in most cases, having children)—what are they celebrating at the wedding ceremony? There are even those who cohabit without any short- or long-term intention of marrying. Either way, cohabiting either simulates marriage or denies it altogether. Cohabiting lacks the fidelity, exclusivity, and permanent stability of marriage. For Christians, cohabiting opposes Christ's redemptive gift of the sacrament that signifies his faithful and indissoluble union with the Church and excludes their participation from those sacraments.

HOLY MATRIMONY IS a sacrament. Like all sacraments, it operates to transform the persons who receive it in Christ. When a man and woman exchange vows before God and the Church, they create a new relationship. The profession of vows unites the Christian man and Christian woman forever in this life as husband and wife as a sign of Christ's love for his bride, the Church.

Words have meaning. The words of the marriage vow hold husband and wife accountable before one another, the witnesses, and before God and the Church. The vows are an act of righteousness as the man and woman entrust themselves to God and one another as Christian disciples.

But if the couple consider themselves already married, what do the vows signify? What difference do they make? Apart from some legal formalities, nothing changes in their relationship. They speak and exchange, then, superfluous or redundant words.

For these couples, the word "cohabitation" replaces the uncomfortably accurate phrase "living in sin." Cohabiting couples might feel insulted by that phrase, but most will find it meaningless. After all, most reject the notion that what they are doing involves sin. But their behavior does not just *involve* sin, an alienation from God; it is truly *living in* sin.

Lady Julia Flyte, a Catholic character from Evelyn Waugh's *Brideshead Revisited*, explains the magnitude and consequences of "living in sin" with her lover compared to her one-time moment of adultery in America:

> "Living in sin"; not just doing wrong, as I did when I went to America; doing wrong, knowing it is wrong, stopping doing it, forgetting. That's not what they mean. . . . *Living in sin*, with sin, by sin, for sin, every hour, every day, year in, year out. Waking up with sin in the morning, seeing the curtains drawn on sin, bathing it, dressing it, clipping diamonds to it, feeding it, showing it round, giving it a good time, putting it to sleep at night with a tablet of Dial if it's fretful.

Instead of living in sin, Jesus Christ calls us to live in him. He seeks to abide in and dwell with us. At the Last Supper, Jesus told his disciples, "Whoever loves me will keep my word, and my Father will love him, and we will come to him and make our dwelling with him" (John 14:23). The righteous man, like Joseph, hears the Word of God and keeps it. He seeks to be with God always. The decision to dwell permanently apart from Jesus—living in sin—leads to death and darkness. We willingly separate ourselves from the source of life, the one who is the Way, the Truth, and the Life. Living in sin is unrighteousness; it is a life in need of healing and forgiveness.

Living in sin—remaining, abiding, dwelling not with Christ, but with sin—is easy. Many couples justify their behavior on the basis of practicalities and economics. Faith, righteousness, grace—these recede into the shadows of more immediate concerns, like paying one rent instead of two or sharing a car.

What is the price of virtue and righteousness? What is the cost of living in grace, abiding and dwelling with Christ? Joseph and Mary were poor, yet they lived apart. As you are beginning to understand, engaged couples striving to put God's will first make the necessary sacrifices and resist the pressures of our secular culture by living apart before the wedding. It is an act of righteousness—especially in our secular hookup culture—for a man deliberately to live apart from his fiancée until they are husband and wife.

THE FIRST CHRISTIANS also struggled to live their faith in
a challenging environment. St. Peter exhorted the Gentile
converts to Christianity to "always be ready to give an explanation to anyone who asks you for a reason for your hope
. . . so that when you are maligned, those who defame your
good conduct in Christ may themselves be put to shame. For
it is better to suffer for doing good, if that be the will of God,
than for doing evil. For Christ also suffered for sins once,
the righteous for the sake of the unrighteous, that he might
lead you to God" (1 Pet. 3:15-18). The word "explanation" in
this verse is a translation of the Greek word *apologia*, which
is also the origin of the word *apology*. Although that term
has come to mean an acknowledgment of wrongdoing, you
probably know that Christians have long used the word *apologist* according to its underlying Greek meaning to describe a
person who defends the Faith against hostile accusations and
opposition.

A righteous man is an apologist. He defends his faith and
his moral actions; he does not apologize (in the modern sense)
for them. A righteous man defends the sanctity of marriage
and of purity. In a sense, St. Joseph was an apologist—not by
anything he wrote or said, but simply by his righteous actions.
Joseph defended God's law and will concerning marriage and
family life. Joseph defended the purity and virginity of Mary
and of himself. Joseph's righteousness concerning his virgin
bride Mary, *the* Virgin, radiates as protector of the Church.
Indeed, Mary, for her part, protected the purity of Joseph.

Theirs was a mutual protection, for the benefit of each and the protection of Jesus.

Joseph, I think you have experienced some of this mutual protection in your growing friendship with Aggie. Your e-mail revealed joy at the beauty and goodness of Aggie, a feminine beauty that triggers a desire to protect rather than to lust. You become angry at the thought of other young men who would take advantage of her or hurl crass sexual innuendo in her direction. The righteous man of God seeks to protect the purity of the women in his life. But too often, men listen to and obey the voice of selfish carnal desires, deaf to the voice of the Good Shepherd calling them to a life of purity, and to a deeper, authentic relationship with a woman.

I am not suggesting that a righteous man must suppress or deny his natural sexual attraction to a woman as evil or sinful. The righteous man is aware of his own desires but restrains them for the sake of what is just and true.

In order to protect the purity and virginity of a woman, a man must first be willing to protect his own purity and virginity. You seem to be learning this truth from your friendship with Aggie. You have described your own growth in virtue and in Christ. Thanks be to God that, most of the time, you no longer feel a need or desire for pornography. This is the fruit of the Holy Spirit guiding you. It is wonderful that you and Aggie text each other after Mass to compare thoughts about the respective homilies and your plans for the rest of the day. Instead of using your phone to sneak in a visit to porn websites, you are using it to grow in your faith and deepen your friendship with Aggie.

The mutual protection of purity and virginity means abiding in Christ, living in grace and not in sin. St. Joseph and the Virgin Mary witnessed to a life of mutual protection centered in Jesus Christ. Catholic couples who cohabit are missing out on the grace and friendship of Christ from the sacraments of marriage and the Eucharist.

In preparation for a life centered in abiding with Christ, men and women must listen to the voice of the Good Shepherd and follow him. Abiding and dwelling with Christ before marriage precludes a man and woman living together. Man and woman are to live in grace, to protect each other's purity, and to guard one another's virginity as Joseph and Mary guarded and protected each other's purity.

Joseph, may you grow in righteousness and be a protector and guardian not only of your own purity, but of the purity of all people, especially women like Aggie.

Know of my prayers for you, especially in the Eucharist.

Abiding with St. Joseph,

Fr. Terry

PS:

—Be a defender and guardian of the Faith by living
  righteously.

—Pray for the grace to suffer hostility and ridicule for your belief in Christ.

—Go to St. Joseph for help with purity!

11

To: **Joseph**

Date: **April 29—St. Catherine of Siena**

Re: **VIRGINITY**

Dear Joseph,

May the joy and wonder of this season of the Resurrection be with you! Easter joy still abounds here in Rome three weeks after the glorious celebration of our Lord's resurrection. After a week of gray clouds and rain, this morning's sunshine and the immaculate sky rejuvenate the heart. The Easter season renews the soul longing for transfiguration, making it glow with freedom and glory. It cannot return to the grave of sin after the risen Lord has revealed the splendor and truth of our sanctification.

The fire of divine love seeks to draw all to its bliss. But our fearful, timid, and selfish human hearts continue to doubt. We fear that when we step out into the abyss, we will fall into nothingness, when in truth we will soar in grace because we've left ourselves behind and have let God permeate and transform us.

With a laptop and a book in hand of the writings of St. Catherine of Siena, I sit before the statue of this four-teenth-century saint whose heart burned to warm the hearts of her contemporaries. She leans forward as she steps, her bare left foot planted on the field of the apostolate, her left hand holding a lily of virginal purity, and her right hand pressed against her heart. The folds of her cloak hide the mystery of a woman whose mission, dignity, and identity are united with her mystical bridegroom, Jesus Christ. Catherine captured the hearts of her people as she tended to nobles, royalty, and even popes, calling them to be faithful. A contemporary of hers said that "no one can escape the charm of this holy virgin."

Yes, St. Catherine was unabashedly a virgin. As you experienced during your college days, many modern young Christians are reluctant to acknowledge their virginity, regarding it as an embarrassing anachronism to eliminate.

I don't need to tell you that the world we live in does not admire deliberate virgins. For the most part, the word does not even appear in popular culture other than in scornful or mocking references. In a society that celebrates carnal indulgence, virgins are strangers and aliens because they neither conform to society nor worship in the sexual temple.

The pressure exists not only at the institutional level of society, but at the personal level of friends and colleagues and peers. Your recent experience at a colleague's party—an environment and mindset that pit the accepted majority against a ridiculed minority—attests to that reality. Imagine—the men gossiped about a particular woman's physical appearance and sexual desirability, and worse, *in the presence of other women*! The obsession with orgasm and contempt for virginity are obvious, especially among the men, who insisted on their "need" for sex. Your colleagues made it clear that they considered sexual activity in any form normal and a life without sex unthinkable.

I can understand how you might leave the party doubting the merits of virginity, wondering if perhaps your colleagues had a point about abstinence as an unnatural and unhealthy repression of sexual desire. After all, these people are smart and sophisticated. You admire their competence and professionalism at work. How could they be wrong on this issue?

Yet, deep down, you know the truth about human sexuality and the human person. You perceived that truth in your uneasiness during your visit last month with your college friend and his girlfriend.

Knowing and living the truth of virginity bring a joy that elevates the entire person. It brings a deeper sense of self and a deeper communion with others than any transitory sexual experience.

ST. CATHERINE WAS irresistibly charming because she dwelt in the truth and spoke the truth. The twenty-fourth of twenty-five children, Catherine was only six when she experienced a mystical vision of Jesus Christ so powerful that she decided to dedicate her life to God. At the age of seven, she made a private vow of virginity to be Christ's bride. At fifteen, Catherine cut her hair in renunciation of her parents' attempt to find her a husband, and at sixteen, this virgin for

Christ openly declared her intention not to marry. After several years of solitude and contemplation, Catherine experienced a mystical espousal to Jesus Christ, who called her out of her solitude into a lifetime of active love of her neighbor. Her life flowed with mystical experiences, extreme fasts and asceticism, prayer, and letters to popes and kings and friends. Catherine referred to God most fondly under variations of Truth: "the First Truth," "gentle First Truth," "supreme eternal Truth."

The Greek word for "truth," *alếtheia*, derives from *alethes*, which means "not veiled" or "not forgotten." It is the opposite of Lethe, the river of forgetfulness in Hades, from which, according to the myth, the dead were required to drink to forget the past of their earthly lives. As human beings, we are captivated by the truth. We seek it, and when we find it, we should not abandon it.

Your experiences over the past few months have led you to this fundamental question: what is the truth of the human person? You are in excellent company. St. Catherine, too, pondered this question in prayer. She understood that humanity makes sense only in relation to God and God's love for us through Jesus Christ in the Holy Spirit. She wrote of God, "Why did you so dignify us? With unimaginable love you looked upon your creatures within your very self, and you fell in love with us. So it was love that made you create us and give us being just so that we might taste your supreme good."

St. Catherine, like all the saints, reveals the splendor of the truth of being human. The saints, during their lives on earth,

are sinful creatures, well aware of their fragile nature but at
the same time constantly and gratefully aware that they are
lovingly created by God and for God. You've recognized that
Aggie shines with a similar light that draws you to recognize
better your own divinely bestowed dignity. As a result your
friendship with Aggie shows more clearly the truth about
men and women and their relationships with one another.
Her presence helps purify your thoughts and clarify your vision.

When we draw near to God, to Truth, we are purified,
but when we separate ourselves from God, from Truth, we
become defiled. During one of her mystical experiences, St.
Catherine received this revelation from God: "I am the fire
that purifies the soul. So the nearer the soul comes to me, the
more pure she will become, and the more she departs from
me, the more unclean she is. This is why worldly folk fall into
such wickedness, because they have left me. But the soul who
unites herself directly with me shares in my own purity."

You asked me how you can truly see another person. St.
Catherine regarded the men and women of her day with love
and in truth. She loved them not on their own, or for themselves, but only in God and for God. This exemplifies the act
of charity: "I love my neighbor as myself for the love of you."
From the age of twenty-one until her death twelve years later,
she abandoned her three years of solitude in prayer at home
and lived an active life of charity and mercy for those in phys-

ical and spiritual need. Knowing that God is "mad with love" for us ignited her love for her neighbor. In Siena, during the famine of 1370 and the plague of 1374, she went through the city tending to the needs of the hungry and the sick and dying. The poor, hungry, and sick flocked to her door, knowing Catherine would help them.

Her union with God and love of him was the basis for her love of neighbor. At the age of six, Catherine had a vision of Jesus, and the next year made a vow of perpetual virginity. At the conclusion of her solitude before being sent out into the world, Catherine experienced a mystical espousal to Christ. He placed a ring on her finger, a betrothal he promised would keep her pure and virgin. From this nuptial relationship with Christ, she possessed the freedom to be truly herself, her virginal self, with others. Catherine's prayer revealed her pure desire for God, the one who truly corresponds to our human longings for union: "You, eternal Trinity, are a deep sea: the more I enter you, the more I discover, and the more I discover, the more I seek you."

In contrast to Catherine's true vision of men and women is a false vision that obscures our relationship to God. This false vision belongs to those who might be called "sensual" men. They lack a true vision because they see others not in relation to God, but only in relation to their own desires.

The sensual man evaluates every woman for her sexual attractiveness. He stares at women he sees on the street and may even call after them with crude suggestions. He will not resist a woman's sexual advances, even if they are both married to other people. He is easily drawn to pornography and regularly indulges in selfish sexual stimulation.

As you know from your own experience, both college dorms and grown-up workplaces are filled with sensual men. They delight in being sensual and consider it normal. But as you have also come to recognize, the sensual man lives a falsehood. His life is based on lies. He can see women only with lust, which addles his mind. He drinks insatiably from the river Lethe, forgetting that he is a creature of God, forgetting the dignity of his identity in God, forgetting the truth.

St. Catherine regarded sensuality as a deviation from God's truth. Suzanne Noffke, a Dominican scholar of St. Catherine, explains that sensuality is "not the simple reality of our being physical, sensate beings; it is rather a perversion of our humanness, an inversion of values, a contradiction of truth and a return to 'the great lie' that denies our relationship with God. It is the self-deception that deludes us into creating our own truth, whether in selfishness or in slavish fear, instead of searching honestly and in love for God's truth."

Joseph, you have come to understand that men must tame their unruly desires so they may attain the objects of their true desire: God and the truth. You've noticed this yourself in your friendship with Aggie: you appreciate her beauty and strive to govern your formerly unruly sexual desires by directing them to the truth of Aggie's dignity as a daughter of God. C.S. Lewis describes our redeemed sexuality as a great stallion that has been transformed from a prior sinful reptilian form. Man and stallion breathe into one another's nostrils. Such is the power and purity of true sexuality and passion, a joy in bodily being. The man of God, who joyfully directs this stallion to a virtuous end, has immense capacity for communion with another person. Heart speaks to heart. Your heart's true desire is to know and love God and know and love one another in him. If you forget or repress your true desire, you will seek after false desires, which ultimately will not satisfy you. You will become like the people of Judah, of whom Jeremiah complains, "Two evils have my people done: they have forsaken me, the source of living waters; they have dug themselves cisterns, broken cisterns, that hold no water" (Jer. 2:13).

Sensual people have forsaken God, yet they still thirst, forgetting that God alone, the fount of truth, can satisfy that thirst. St. Catherine explained it well:

> If you have received my love sincerely without self-interest, you will drink your neighbor's love sincerely. It is just like a vessel that you fill at the fountain. If you take it out of the fountain to drink, the vessel is soon empty. But if you hold your vessel in the fountain while you drink, it will not get empty: indeed it will always be full. So the love of your neighbor, whether spiritual or temporal, is meant to be drunk in me, without any self-interest.

You have been honest in acknowledging the struggle involved in turning away from your false but relentlessly powerful sensual desires to seek your dignity as a son of God and the even more relentless power of his love. Aggie has been a tremendous positive influence, but this is not a battle that can be won overnight.

Don't be discouraged that your sincere desire to live a virtuous life has not instantly transformed you into a saint. Just keep bringing your vessel to the fountain. God will never tire of refilling it. Or like St. Catherine says, immerse the vessel, yourself, in the fountain of God. Rely totally on him. St. Catherine, too, was well aware of the extent to which she fell short of the glory of God, but she persisted in prayer and constantly turned back to the infinite love of God:

> The more I gaze upon your exaltedness in the Word's Passion, the more my poor wretched soul is ashamed of never having known you—and this because I have been continually alive to my sensuality's affection, and dead to reason. But today may your charity's exaltedness be pleased to enlighten the eye of my understanding, and that of those you have given me as my children, and that of every reasoning creature.

The sensual man can see only dimly. He recognizes only a woman's body. He forgets the truth of human dignity, both his and hers. The man of truth, by contrast, sees the whole person of the woman before him. He regards her in light of God, who is her Creator, in light of her redemption by the crucified Jesus Christ, in light of her dignity as the dwelling place of the Holy Spirit. He delights in her whole being, seeks only her good, and with purity of heart looks into her heart. He is thus able to enter into true union and communion with her.

Joseph, Catherine proclaimed the truth of virginity. I am praying that you be a truth-teller by your chaste witness to

God's love for you, praying that all men be enflamed by God's blazing love and so live true lives—seeing women not with lust, but with a singular vision of truth and love.

Know of my prayers for you, especially in the Eucharist, united with Jesus Christ.

In the truth of God and Easter joy,

Fr. Terry

PS:

—Govern and transform your sexual thoughts by being always mindful of the truth about women's dignity.

—Let your chaste words and actions shine the light of truth in a world made dim by lust.

—Only God can satisfy and fulfill your desires!

12

To: **Joseph**

Date: **May 24—Pentecost**

Re: **LIFE IN THE SPIRIT**

Dear Joseph,

May the fire of the Holy Spirit be with you on this Pentecost, so that you may boldly proclaim and live the truth of the gospel of Jesus Christ! As the Holy Spirit descended like tongues of flame upon the disciples in the upper room on Pentecost, filling them with the power to proclaim the crucified and risen Lord, so too does the Spirit embolden and sanctify us as members of the Church to spread the good news. The apostles and disciples burst forth from the isolated security of that room to set the world ablaze as Jesus had so desired (Luke 12:49). They were filled with boldness—*parresia*, a Greek word that also means daring, trust, confidence, firmness, constancy, and perseverance. People marveled at the *boldness* of Peter and John (Acts 4:13); the house where the disciples gathered was shaken as they prayed; they proclaimed the word of God *boldly* (Acts 4:31); and Paul and Barnabas spoke *boldly* in the Lord (Acts 14:3).

The risen and exalted Lord Jesus Christ pours out divine love, the Holy Spirit, received from the Father, upon the disciples that forms them into the Church, the Body of Christ and temple of the Holy Spirit. Love, the Holy Spirit, unites them and draws them into the communion of love of the Trinity. Filled with this divine love, the disciples are faithful to the teaching of and communion with the apostles, to the Eucharist, and to the prayers (Acts 2:42). The risen Jesus has ascended to the right hand of the Father but is still present with the disciples, most wonderfully in his sacramental and real presence in the Eucharist. Because of the Resurrection, Jesus can be present to all people, not just to a few as in our case or in his pre-resurrection state. Though not a physical presence, Jesus Christ is present bodily in a more deeply bodily way—in his resurrected and glorified body. The Holy Spirit makes us new creations in Christ and empowers us to live our bodily life with boldness.

The Spirit lifts us beyond our ordinary, natural existence and transforms us into spiritual persons—not by destroying our humanity or bodiliness, but by perfecting them. St. Paul contrasts the natural person (*psychikos anthropos*), who in his folly neither understands nor accepts what pertains to the Spirit of God, and the spiritual person, who is open to receive the Spirit and knows the mind of God (1 Cor. 2:14-15). In baptism, our very bodies are temples of the Holy Spirit who dwells within us. The Spirit enables us to worship God truly and reverently and to be holy. Permeated by the Holy Spirit, we are to glorify God in and through our bodies, as St. Paul tells the Corinthians (1 Cor. 6:20).

Joseph, your vivid account of Aggie's college graduation weekend reveals that you have truly been living as a man of God, a *pneumatikos anthropos*. I think this is the first time in your e-mails that you have described to me the beauty of flowers and trees! The natural beauty of the campus in May, and the genuine warmth you experienced with Aggie and her family, reminds me of what the Roman Canon (the First Eucharistic Prayer) calls a *locum refrigerii*—literally a "place of refreshment." In the Mass, the term refers to the happiness of the faithful departed who are in the presence of Christ at the heavenly banquet, of which the Eucharist is a participation and foretaste. To be in the presence of Christ is to be in a place of refreshment. The campus was certainly a place of refreshment for you, as you walked with Aggie around the lakes!

The real presence of Jesus Christ in the Eucharist, too, is a place of refreshment that heals and elevates us as we enter into communion with him and with his Body, the Church. The unity and communion of all in the Church and the Eucharist is the fruit of Pentecost and the Spirit's love. This communion with Christ in the Eucharist is the pattern for our human relationships where we encounter another heart to heart. The real, personal presence of another deepens our humanity. But at the same time, physical presence alone does not reveal the total person of another. After all, we can be squeezed next to other people on a commuter train or a long flight without even knowing their names, let alone their interior thoughts. And, as you know from being around your peers, people can engage in intimate sexual activities with virtual strangers, never bothering with anything but superficial conversation (if that). The truth of another human person remains hidden until we enter into a relationship of trust and communion. Such a relationship allows us to receive as a gift what the other person offers, and you are building that sort of relationship with Aggie.

YOU WROTE ABOUT your longing to see Aggie since your last visit a few months ago, and the various ways in which you stay in touch with her to assuage that longing. Phone calls, e-mails, text messages—these are wonderful ways of communicating with friends, but they are not the same as being together in the same room. Even video chat, which lets you *pretend* to be in the same room, is a poor substitute for the real thing.

Through most of the twentieth century, when the internet was a dream and long-distance phone calls were expensive, friends separated by distance were forced to rely on letters to keep in touch—literally, for a letter from a friend is a tangible, material expression of that friend's person. It is wonderful that Aggie persuaded you to exchange letters in addition to your more frequent electronic communication. You mentioned the joy you experienced in holding the same piece of paper Aggie had also touched, on which she had written a special message by hand, and that sometimes even contained a hint of her perfume. Aggie's letters to you, and yours to her, are tangible, material expressions of your persons. They enable you to have a form of communion, even though it is separated by time and space, that is impossible with electronic devices.

Although you treasure the letters from Aggie, you've admitted that you also treasure your phone, that marvelous device that allows you to call, text, or e-mail Aggie for an immediate connection. If she's not available, you can look at her picture until she gets back to you. So I understand your distress when your phone suddenly stopped working and you had to wait two days for a replacement. We have all become accustomed to the immediate availability offered by our smartphones, and a malfunctioning phone or the unexpected lack of Wi-Fi leaves us with a sense of isolation and abandonment.

But have you noticed that this greater capacity for communication may lead to greater alienation from personal contact and communion? Surely you've had the experience of being with someone who is present but not present *to you* because he is glued to his phone. Perhaps you have sometimes been that person who is too busy texting to respond to a question from the friend sitting beside you. Many families will text one another at home because it is less disruptive than shouting (the pretext) and much easier than getting up and walking to another room (the real reason).

With their instantaneous reach across space, text messages facilitate communication, but they can also push people away. Compared to a handwritten letter, texting and e-mail introduce more levels of separation between the participants. You can't see your friend's unique handwriting; you certainly can't smell perfume.

Though technology allows us instantly to communicate with people across the globe, many of us may rarely speak to our next-door neighbors. It is possible for us to lose the ability to interact with a living human being face to face as we spend increasing amounts of time on our devices.

You are well aware that no substitute exists for the real presence of Aggie you encountered last Saturday. You cannot replace personal presence and communion with a video recording or live webcam image. No virtual reality comes close to walking around a lake with one you love. No substitute exists for the Real Presence of Christ, either. Catholicism is vacuous if the risen Lord is not really present in the Eucharist.

IMMERSION INTO THE virtual world endangers the truth of our embodied existence, which is our real, personal existence. It tempts many men away from real relationships and the real presence of others. This is evident with video games, social media, smartphones, and other electronic devices. The virtual world of video games, with their increasingly realistic graphics, can captivate boys and men for hours. It is easy to see how the virtual world, created purely for entertainment, becomes more interesting than the actual world, with its complications and demands and responsibilities. You recognize this truth from your own experience, when you and your college roommates would play yet another round of *Halo* instead of getting down to studying for finals, or when you couldn't pry your young nephews away from their screens when it was time for Christmas dinner. We can enter into a virtual world as we might enter into the imaginary world of a book of fiction, but the virtual world provides immediate interaction that a book does not.

I contend with students who are so accustomed to interacting through social media and academic electronic platforms that they are averse to and even feel threatened by direct conversation with fellow students in the classroom, especially if there is disagreement among positions. Interface communication diminishes modern dating as well. Asking someone in person to go on a date, or even calling the person and having to make your intentions known, requires a self-revelation manifest in some kind of bodily form presented to the other—eye contact, pounding heart, spoken voice, nervous behavior, sweat, etc. Texting and e-mail hide or eliminate most of this self-revelation.

More impersonal and also dehumaninzing and morally corrupt is the virtual world of pornography. You encountered a vivid example of the power of the virtual world to lure men away from reality during your visit to the airport bar before your flight last weekend. Those two men at the table near the restroom, both wearing wedding rings but obviously watching porn on a phone, were allowing themselves to engage in sexual fantasies with the graphic images of nameless women instead of talking with or thinking about their wives. They immersed themselves in the inner world of their own fantasies, deliberately stirring their passions, gazing lustfully at the women on the screen. As you rightly observed, these women were not personally present. Only an image was presented rather than the fullness of their very real wives at home.

These men were pusillanimous, a vice in which one, be-cause of a small soul, shrinks away from great things. Pusil-lanimity is small-mindedness, a cowardice of character that leads a man to reject the responsibilities and demands before him. The pusillanimous man is not a man of God. The former has the power to respond, but he will not exert himself. He fears failure and so refuses to grow, to challenge himself, to extend his abilities. He indulges in his passions and remains at the level of the natural man without the Spirit—or even at the level of an animal—rather than rising to the greatness of which he is capable, the level of personhood that respects and reverences the dignity of a woman. In Jesus' parable of the talents, in which the master entrusts to his servants varying amounts of wealth, the pusillanimous servant is the one who buries his single talent in the ground while the others, who received larger amounts, double their master's money. The servant refrains from action because he is fearful of the fu-ture encounter with his master, who will judge him on what the servant doubts he can accomplish. The pusillanimous man buries himself in the virtual world of pornography, fearful of engaging the real bodily presence of a woman.

Joseph, I commend you for your magnanimous engage-ment of the real presence of Aggie last week. Through your behavior, you lived up to the dignity of the woman beside you. In contrast to the pusillanimous men at the airport bar, who profaned both the unknown women on the porn web-site and their wives, you honored and reverenced both Aggie's body and your own.

YOU MIGHT RECALL the words of St. Paul in his letter to the Corinthians: "Do you not know that your body is a temple of the Holy Spirit within you?" (1 Cor. 6:19). At first glance, this comparison seems extreme. The word "temple" calls to mind an elaborate building—the Mormon temple in Salt Lake City or the Jedi temple in the *Star Wars* movies—rather than a mere human body. But for the people of Israel, the temple in Jerusalem was the place where the One God dwelt. God's presence (the *Shekinah*) was there. In the temple, no profane or mundane actions took place. In the presence of God, human personhood deepened as people entered into an intimate relationship with God.

Paul compared the body to a temple because some of the members of the Church thought the body was of lesser or no importance compared to the soul. Because they assumed that the body had no bearing on salvation, they concluded that they could do whatever they wanted in and with their bodies. Some of the Corinthians engaged in prostitution and other promiscuous sexual behavior. Paul condemned such behavior as a denigration of the body that profaned the person in the same way that improper behavior within the temple desecrated it. Their very bodily gestures spoke a language that was profane and immoral.

Paul exhorted the Corinthians to avoid *porneia*, the Greek word meaning "immorality" and the root of the term "pornography." *Porneia* means unchastity, and indeed any kind of sexual immorality such as fornication and prostitution. More broadly, Paul's words condemned any kind of profanation of one's own or another's body.

Your body—your person—is the temple of the Holy Spirit. Our bodily lives should reverence and respect the dignity of who we are as the very dwelling place of God. Whether through chastity, friendship, or merciful shown love to the poor, the suffering, and the marginalized, we can bear witness to how we rejoice in the embodiedness of ourselves and others. We are, in the words of St. Paul, to glorify God in our bodies (1 Cor. 6:20).

Joseph, I have noticed a certain boldness emerging in you over these last months as you are learning to glorify God in your body as you have been responding with grace to the real, personal, bodily presence of Aggie. Moved by the Spirit, you have matured in faith—a faith that is strengthened when it is shared. Through your actions, even more than your words, you can be an apostle to your friends to help them see the truth of a spiritual man, a man of God. We need spiritual men to live with a new boldness in our anointed embodiedness. "For those who are led by the spirit of God are sons of God. For you did not receive a spirit of slavery to fall back into fear, but you received a spirit of adoption, through whom we cry, 'Abba, Father!'" (Rom. 8:11-15). Your e-mails these last few months reveal a freedom in the Spirit compared to a former slavery to sinful passions. Isn't this the freedom of personal contact with Aggie, and also with God?

Know of my prayers for you and Aggie, especially in the Eucharist, where we are united by the Spirit into the one Body of Christ, the Church.

Come, Holy Spirit,

Fr. Terry

PS:

—Put down your phone, close your laptop, and choose to live in the real, embodied world of persons and experiences.

—Honor the body as much as the soul: it is the temple of God.

—Be a great-souled man, living boldly in the Holy Spirit!

13

To: **Joseph**

Date: **July 14—St. Kateri Tekakwitha**

Re: **COURTSHIP**

Dear Joseph,

The Lord be with you on this memorial of the first Native American saint! I celebrated Mass this morning with our summer pilgrimage group from the university at the Shrine of the North America Martyrs. This is where the Jesuit priest Isaac Jogues and two Jesuit oblates, René de Goupil and Jean de Lalande, were martyred in the seventeenth century by the Mohawks. Ten years after their deaths, Kateri was born at this same location along the confluence of Schoharie Creek and the Mohawk River. The blood of the martyrs blossomed into the woman known as the Lily of the Mohwaks.

In the restful quiet of the woods and farmland of this area, I've been re-reading your e-mail about a most wonderful development between you and Aggie: a first kiss. Secretly, I had been wondering if your friendship would transform itself like this (and from what you said about her family's reaction, I

wasn't alone). What happened over the Fourth of July weekend when you were visiting her in St. Paul was the outward
manifestation of what has been germinating inwardly for
some time. In the freshness and freedom of a weekend away
from work and in the context of your comfort with the Culross family, you started to see Aggie with a heart awakening to
the truth of your enjoyment and delight in her.

This only increased Saturday morning, when she picked
you up early to begin a tour of the Twin Cities, beginning
with the country's first basilica: the co-cathedral of St. Mary
in Minneapolis. Later you drove around the chain of lakes
region with its upscale neighborhoods and lacustrine beauty
that draws so many Minnesotans outdoors. The whole time,
you had a heightened sense of her presence. Each incidental
contact between you as you walked through the basilica to
stop to look at stained glass windows or the statutes of the
apostles became an unspoken deliberate action initiated by
both of you and resisted by neither. I can believe it that you
spent less time looking out the window at the lakes than at
her as she drove, attentive to every detail about her. As you
walked along a path above the Mississippi River, you were
aware of Aggie's bodily presence, attentive to every detail—
the scent of her hair, the timbre of her voice, the shapeli-
ness of her figure, the sparkle of her hazel eyes, the radiating
joy of her smile, the lightness of her step, all of which em-
bodying her cheerfulness, vibrant faith, love of God, humility,
graciousness, devotedness to her family and friends, merciful
heart, and yearning for justice. You were quite the gentleman
as you took her arm in yours and walked downhill along the

path: two persons encountering each other heart to heart.

What prompted you to ask, as you stood at the overlook gazing upon the great river below, "May I kiss you?" But I commend you for it. It raised the level of engagement and situated your embrace within the context of freedom and personhood. Your waiting for a response acknowledged her as a person.

You were not in a bubble. It was not just the two of you separated and isolated from other relationships and responsibilities. You and Aggie joined Steve and Marie at their home for dinner Saturday night and were immersed in the family dinner Sunday afternoon after Mass in the morning. Though you would have liked to be alone with her, it was wise of her not to bring you to her apartment except when she took you there with her brother Steve to pick something up for the dinner.

AND THEN YOU thought of her the whole trip back to Chicago. Being separated by 400 miles presents challenges when you want to see someone every day! Your plan to visit her for a weekend once a month sounds good; it was kind of her parents and brother to offer you a place to stay. Her plan to visit you at the end of this month is trickier. Without family in the area, your options are limited. How about the older single woman from the parish you mentioned you have met a couple of times?

It's too bad that your parish can't be of more help to you and others in facilitating chaste courtship. (And Joseph, let's recognize that courtship is more than dating. Christian men and women *court* in order to discern whether to marry each other. You're not merely having fun and getting to know one another; you're discovering the other's true character and identity in Christ.) I think the parish community has a role to play—for example, by opening their homes to those who are courting (or who are engaged) long-distance. This would help restore a sense of parochial communal *belonging* and responsibility among Catholics. Courtship and engagement are not supposed to be self-enclosed relationships, rather they should be embedded within the life of the parish community. Parishioners have responsibility for one another; we are our brother's keepers.

What your co-workers consider old-fashioned and restraining when you told them about these housing plans has, being *truth*-fashioned, allowed you to get to know Aggie in the context of her family. You've learned about *eros* love in the context of many other kinds of family love—that of parents, sibling, in-laws, cousins, and uncles and aunts—and *agape*, Christian love, as you prayed before meals, visited her sick grandmother, went to Mass on Sunday morning, and shared in the Sunday mid-afternoon family dinner before driving back to Chicago.

For centuries, couples grew in their relationship immersed in the culture of the Church. Family and friends helped the young man and woman exercise chastity and modesty. Chaperones accompanied the couple so that they were not alone when together. Chaperones helped form the consciences of the young man and woman by being a physical reminder of the communal and social dimensions of their relationship. The chaperones were representative of the communally held expectation that men and women were to reserve sex for marriage. Their presence helped the man and woman tame their passions. Today, many Christians readily make the decision to cohabit or engage in the *marital* act before their wedding. The cultural context has shifted, and either the Church's communal expectations are not declared or they are ignored as something medieval. An individualistic and relativistic morality has arisen.

Living a Christian life, particularly as a courting couple, is difficult in our modern culture. Couples face constant pressure to conform to licentious societal norms. St. Kateri faced similar pressure as the only Christian in the Mohawk village. The daughter of a Mohawk chief and a Christian Algonquin mother, Kateri was orphaned at age four due to a smallpox outbreak that left her partially blind in one eye. She was raised by her uncle and aunt.

As the daughter of a chief, Kateri was a prime prospect for marriage, but she refused any advances because of a personal vow of virginity—something unheard of among the Mohawks. She had learned of Catholicism from her mother and wanted to become a Catholic herself. Opposition to Kateri increased after her baptism in 1676, when she was twenty years old. Members of the tribe greeted her with laughter, mockery, and obscene gestures. But they also knew that this "mystic of the wilderness," who preferred solitude and prayer to marriage, lived a life beyond reproach.

Around the same time as Kateri's persecution, Catholics

were being persecuted in England. From the reign of Queen Elizabeth to that King George III, a little over 200 years, Catholics who refused to attend the state's official church services were convicted as "recusants" and suffered fines, seizure of property or land, and exclusion from certain professions. Recusants' names were published on public lists, and they were ostracized.

I think that those who live a chaste courtship today are like those recusants, socially convicted by the world for not participating in its state sexual religion. Chaste courters are strangers and aliens to a society that worships carnal indulgence. The world's propaganda machine—media, scientists, "health" professionals, the entertainment industry, and government officials—promotes and teaches a way of life that celebrates sexual activity outside of marriage. A young man and woman in a chaste courtship are to be ridiculed as Kateri was, and not accepted as full members of society. They are apostates in need of conversion.

You have already faced some of this mindset and opposition. For many of your peers, dating is a preliminary form of marriage, a quasi-marriage that gives them access to marital acts but is not marriage. Even engaged couples are not married couples, just as seminarians are not yet deacons or priests. Although marriage does not involve an ontological change and the conferral of an indelible spiritual character as ordination does, it is still a covenant that creates a fundamentally new and different relationship between a man and a woman. A seminarian may yearn to preside at the Eucharist or to forgive sins, but if he attempted to do these things before ordination he would only *simulate* their reality. (He would also commit a grave offense.) He lacks the Holy Spirit's gift of a sacred power to exercise this ministry.

Likewise, couples who before marriage participate in the marital act only simulate the marriage covenant. Their *anticipation* is not *consummation*. They have not received the Holy Spirit in the sacrament, who is the seal of their marriage covenant and who is the communion of love of Christ and the Church (look in your *Catechism*, #1624). There is no practicing for what courtship is ultimately directed toward: marriage and its consummation in sexual love. Courtship is not minor league baseball, where players work on their skills until they get called up to the big leagues!

You and Aggie are starting to court and that could blossom into marriage. Remain steadfast in your faith and in your chaste relations with Aggie. Court her like a man of God.

YOU AND AGGIE are both committed to chastity and not having sex before marriage, but questions will arise about the exact boundaries of physical intimacy. In these times, remember your duty to protect one another's hearts. Be aware of your own passions and desires; don't treat them lightly, no matter how pure your intentions. When you're visiting one another, give yourselves a curfew and honor it. (*Curfew* derives from the French words meaning "to cover a fire," which referred to the extinguishing of fires at a fixed time at night. Cover the fires of any passions that can be enflamed by being together too long into the night!) Keep the bedroom off limits; it should be a sanctuary of solitude and modesty. When traveling, as with the wedding you have both been invited to, stay in separate hotel rooms and keep the curfew.

On the positive side: celebrate the sacraments. Go to Mass together when you can and to reconciliation regularly. Pray together. Do service work together. Spend time with married couples who live the Faith. Learn from them firsthand how they integrate work, family life, faith, and their love for one another. If you have friends with young children, volunteer to babysit for them together with Aggie. You will learn about how both of you relate to children.

Go on inexpensive but creative dates that are not passive but active. Instead of going to a movie where you sit watching a screen, go for walks, play games, engage one another. I encourage you to be outdoors. St. Kateri is the patronness of ecology and the environment. Creation and redemption are part of God's single plan of salvation. All things are created in and through the Word of God, Jesus Christ, who was incarnate of the Virgin Mary. Go out together into creation—whether a botanical garden, or county or state parks—and encounter God the Creator through his creation. Gaze at the stars together—more effective when visiting her, of course—and ponder the mystery of God who gives each of them a name (Psalm 147:4). Learn to identify the grammar of creation present in all things, including yourselves, in your givenness as man and woman. Courtship subordinates itself to God's nuptial design for men and women who are ordered to one another.

As you court her, engage her heart to heart. Hand-write

notes to her—on paper—that affirm her and express your thoughts and feelings about her. Be modest and chaste in word and deed. Be tender and be honorable. Because it's so powerful, physical intimacy can threaten to displace other kinds of intimacy: spiritual, intellectual, emotional, familial. Keep this in mind as you move forward in courting Aggie. At the moment, you are caught up in the wonder of knowing her. Your love for her encompassed her whole being in her radical uniqueness. Your response to her reminds me of Tobias from the Book of Tobit. I have always liked the translation from the Jerusalem Bible: "he fell so deeply in love with her that he could no longer call his heart his own" (6:18). It expresses your sense of belonging to one another. You are no longer your own person. As a man of God, you encounter her heart to heart, and your heart belongs to her and hers to you. But they both belong to Christ's Sacred Heart.

Joseph, may St. Kateri be a guide for you in this delightful time. Know of my prayers for you and Aggie, especially in the Eucharist.

In Christ's love,

Fr. Terry

PS:

—Remember that courtship is not inward-looking but embraces the love of family, community, and Christ.

—Pray together for the grace to protect each other's garden in chastity and to be faithful witnesses in an unchaste world.

—You have learned to let your heart speak to another. Now learn to give your heart away!

Postscript

To: **Joseph**

Date: **October 17—St. Ignatius of Antioch**

Re: **PERSISTENT MOTIVATION**

Dear Joseph,

Joyful greetings in the risen Lord on this day before the baptism of your first child, Luke Francis. I am disappointed that my Baltimore conference obligations prevent me from being with you and Aggie and your families and friends in Chicago tomorrow, but I am glad that Luke will be baptized by his uncle, Fr. Pete. I very much enjoyed their company at your wedding a year and a half ago!

My seminary lodgings are not far from the Cathedral of Mary Our Queen, where I spent some time in quiet prayer this morning. The stained glass window of Noah's ark high on the north wall above the sanctuary struck me. The ark, seen straight on, is in motion, ploughing the water ahead, rainbow and dove with olive branch depicted above the vessel. I think I was drawn to contemplate that image because it is a type or symbol of the Church and of baptism. At the baptism tomorrow, Fr. Pete will bless the water in the font and say, "The waters of the great Flood you made a sign of the waters of baptism, that make an end of sin and a new beginning of goodness." God washed away the sins of humankind with the waters of the Flood, and Noah and his wife with their three sons and their wives began humanity anew. The ark with its eight holy people is a type of the Church as the people of God washed clean in the waters of baptism.

The typology of the ark and Church was a common theme among the early Fathers of the Church. The ark is one as the Church is one. There was not a fleet of arks, but just the one. There is only one Church, and it subsists in the Catholic Church. There is "one Lord, one faith, one baptism, one God and Father of all, who is over all and through all and in all" (Eph. 4:5-6). Noah and his family entered the ark through the one door in the side. Christians enter the Church through the side of Christ. In John's Gospel, the soldier pierced the side of Christ on the cross just after he had died, and blood and water flowed out (19:34). Blood and water are the two sacraments of baptism and the Eucharist. These sacraments of the Church originate from Christ. The wood of the ark is the wood of the Cross.

God instructed Noah to construct the ark with three decks (Gen.6:16). One spiritual interpretation of these three levels is the three levels of spiritual perfection: purgation, illumination, and perfection (or union). Purgation is confession of and turning away from sins, illumination is lifting one's mind to God, and perfection is union with God in love. Noah makes the ark with gopherwood and seals it with pitch, inside and out. He does not use nails. The glutinous pitch holds the ark together, a symbol of the love that holds the Church together. Once Noah and his family enter the ark, God "shut[s] him in" (Gen. 7:16). God closes the door. He is the one who makes sure the family is secure and safe aboard the ark that will save them from destruction. As St. Augustine writes in the *City of God*, "this is certainly a figure of the city of God sojourning in this world; that is to say, of the Church, which is rescued by the wood on which hung the mediator of God and men, the man Christ Jesus." The ark in the stained glass window is moving forward toward a destination. It is on a journey. The ark, like the Church, is sojourning. A *sojourner* is one who resides in a place temporarily as a way station on a journey or pilgrimage. St. Augustine's fifth-century words continue the theological imagery of the anonymous mid-second century Christian writer who described the martyrdom of St. Polycarp, the bishop of Smyrna: "The church of God that sojourns at Smyrna to the church of God that sojourns at Philomelium, and to all those of the holy and Catholic Church who sojourn in every place." Smyrna and Philomelium were local churches, as with those of Ephesus, Philippi, and Corinth to which Paul wrote letters, that have their modern equivalents in the dioceses of Chicago and Baltimore.

All of these churches are sojourning in those local places. Chicago is not the final destination; it is a way station. As you and Aggie prepare to have Luke Francis baptized tomorrow at St. Michael parish, form your family identity and mission around the reality that you are sojourners. *Sojourn* is related to the word *parish,* which comes from the Greek word for an alien or stranger. In the First Letter of St. Peter, the author exhorts his readers, "Beloved, I beg you as aliens (*paroikous*) and exiles to abstain from the passions of the flesh that wage war against your soul" (2:11). *Paraoikos* is one who lives as a temporary dweller around (*para*) someone's house (*oikos*). We get the word *parochial* from *para-oikos*. It refers to a parish and, literally, to a stranger. You, Aggie, Luke Francis, and I are all strangers on earth; "our homeland is in heaven" (Phil. 3:20). We live as resident aliens in this world with a burning desire for our true home. Baptizing Luke Francis tomorrow, you bring him onto the ark through the side door—the side of Christ—and journey together toward our heavenly home.

FORM YOUR FAMILY life around your parish and being a sojourner. Know and be known explicitly as a *Catholic* family. The saint whom we celebrated today, St. Ignatius of Antioch, was the bishop of Antioch and martyred in Rome around the year 117. As guards forced him to travel from Antioch to Rome, he wrote seven letters to six local churches and to Polycarp. The seven letters he wrote en route to his martyrdom are a masterpiece of early Christian theology, including the first recorded reference to the Catholic Church: "You should regard that Eucharist as valid which is celebrated either by the bishop or by someone he authorizes. Where the bishop is present, there let the congregation gather, just as where Jesus Christ is, there is the Catholic Church" (*Smyrnaeans*, 8:2). St. Ignatius eagerly anticipated his martyrdom and being with Christ, describing his own upcoming death in eucharistic terms: "I am God's wheat, and I am being ground by the teeth of wild beasts to make a pure loaf for Christ" (Rom. 4:2). The Eucharist was central to his life, not only as a participation in the life of Christ but also as a communion with the Church. The bishop also writes about the Virgin Mary, emphasizing the true humanity of Jesus through her. He explicitly refers to Mary's virginity and her giving birth to Jesus, mysteries "that escaped the notice of the prince of this world" (Eph. 19:1).

Permeating these treasured letters from the early Church is Ignatius' explicit sense of his Christian identity as a man of God, a man of Christ, and a man of the Church. He is firm and resolute, uncompromising in his fidelity: "It is not that I want merely to be called a Christian, but actually to *be* one" (Rom. 3:2). This identity of faith is not temporary but permanent: "For what matters is not a momentary act of professing but being persistently motivated by faith" (Eph. 14:2). Joseph, you and Aggie will be asked tomorrow at the doors of St. Michael's church about your being "persistently motivated by faith" as you prepare to raise Luke Francis as a Catholic.

You and Aggie are Luke's first teachers in the ways of the Faith. You will have many people, in your families and in the Church, to assist you in this lifelong undertaking, but you and Aggie bear primary responsibility. You are handing on the Faith to the next generation as it has been handed on for 2,000 years and was handed on to you. Pope Francis wrote in his first encyclical, "The transmission of the Faith not only brings light to men and women in every place; it travels through time,

passing from one generation to another. Because faith is born
of an encounter which takes place in history and lights up our
journey through time, it must be passed on in every age. It is
through an unbroken chain of witnesses that we come to see
the face of Jesus" (*Lumen Fidei* 38). Luke Francis will come
to encounter Christ through the two of you and through the
Christian life that begins in baptism. Baptism is not just an
event for one day, but for a lifetime of continued encounters
with Christ through the profession of faith, celebration of
the liturgy, prayer, and the sanctification of your ordinary life.

The Creed that you profess every Sunday is also called
the "symbol of faith." The word *symbol* comes from a Greek
verb that means "to come together" or "to throw together."
It refers to two halves of an object, such as a ring or medal-
lion, being reunited, as when two separated parties mutually
identify the other as trustworthy or as belonging to the same
mission because of the restoration of the unity of the broken
object. When you go to Mass, each of you professes, "*I* believe
in one God . . ." You and Aggie bring your own symbol, or
individual piece of the whole, that fits together into the one
Faith. Through the symbol, you and all those present mutually recognize each other and form a unity. You belong to one
another because you all belong to Christ. You are all on the
one ark. The profession of the Creed reminds you where you
originated and where you are headed.

Prayer is essential to your relationship with one another in
Christ. Prayer is foundational for every Catholic family. You
and Aggie will be the first to teach Luke to pray, to know
and love God. I encourage you in your decision to teach

Luke, when he is old enough, the *Shema*: "Hear, O Israel! The Lord is our God, the Lord alone! Therefore, you shall love the Lord, your God, with your whole heart, and with your whole being, and with your whole strength" (Deut. 6:4-5). Jesus identified this as the first commandment, and to love your neighbor as yourself as the second. In preparation for teaching Luke, you and Aggie have been praying these words every morning and night, as Deuteronomy continues: "Keep repeating them to your children. Recite them when you are at home and when you are away, when you lie down and when you get up" (6:6-7). I also exhort you and Aggie to continue to devote ten to fifteen minutes each day in silent contemplative prayer in solitude where you are alone with God.

Just as monasteries have an *horarium*, or schedule of hours for the day's activities, you can create a family *horarium* to govern your family activities. You want to be deliberate in forming a Catholic identity for Luke and all the children God gives you. Besides the *Shema*, and praying before meals, pray the *Angelus* each evening at 6 pm or at dinner. Since every Friday is a day of penance in the Church, abstain from meat as your default penance unless circumstances demand a change. Pray the rosary together at least on Saturdays, the day dedicated to Mary. On Sunday, the Lord's Day, observe this day of rest by refraining from unnecessary work, from shopping (even online), and from electronic entertainment. You want to be refreshed by going out into Creation—for example, by going to a park, to the lake, to the arboretum—or by going on a spiritual pilgrimage, such as visiting a shrine. You also want to develop the tradition of having Sunday dinner with extended family.

All the while, of course, you must balance the regular order of an *horarium* with the fluidity of life that comes with a baby's unscheduled demands! But the creed, the sacraments, and prayer will fuel your efforts to put your faith into daily practice in your ordinary life. Your faith is not something private to be kept behind closed doors. It is about who you are and what you do—in the world. You and Aggie, as a lay man and woman, live in the world, and you are to be like leaven, transforming the world from within it. The "world" encompasses all those aspects of your daily life—work and social and family life. You and Aggie, as part of the Church, are a sign of the invisible kingdom of God. In the midst of a relentlessly secular culture, remember that you are a tangible, bodily, and effective sign of God's kingdom of love, mercy, and justice. You are called to *be* holy and to *make the world* holy.

WE'LL HAVE TO have a phone conversation about your question concerning your resources and the poor. Ever since your visit to the Catholic Worker, you and Aggie have been praying about and discussing the principles of Catholic social teaching—the common good, universal destination of goods, subsidiarity, participation, and solidarity—in relation to how you should practice the corporal works of mercy: feed the hungry, clothe the naked, shelter the homeless, etc. You feel the Lord is calling you to respond more intentionally to his teaching that what we do to our brothers and sisters we do to him (Matt. 25:31-46). Scripture teaches that "life's prime needs are

water, bread, and clothing, and also a house for decent privacy" (Sir. 29:21). I look forward to future conversations about
how what you identify as secondary or tertiary "needs" relates
to those who live without "prime needs." But remember that
the parents of a newborn get daily opportunities to feed the
hungry and clothe the naked!

Responsive to the life of grace, you and Aggie and Luke as
a Catholic family are to make your community more worthy
of God. This includes not only your relationships with others,
especially the poor, but also with Creation itself. Pope Francis
added an eighth corporal and spiritual work of mercy: care for
God's Creation. Spiritually, we are to gratefully contemplate
it, and corporally, we are to break with violent, exploitive, and
selfish ecological actions and instead treat our temporal home
with care and mercy so as to offer it as something beautiful
to God. On the ark are all the animals. After the flood waters
receded, God made a covenant, signified by the rainbow, not
only with humankind but with every living creature (Gen.
9:9-10). You and Aggie are to recognize yourselves foremost
as creatures who have a relationship to the Creator, to one
another, and to all other creatures. Made in the image of God,
your care for your own selves, one another, Luke, and Creation itself should manifest the mercy of the crucified Christ,
who wore a crown of thorns, not a crown of gold.

You enter into this creaturely identity also through your
embrace of natural family planning, respecting God's order
and the limits of your human will. You have frankly admitted
that periodic abstinence has been a sacrifice for both of you,
but you understand that it is an act of faith that strengthens

and deepens your personal encounter and trust of one another and of God. You share this sacrifice together through
prayer, honest dialogue, and reverence for the other. Ignore
the disdain and mockery you and Aggie sometimes receive
from peers, even in the parish, who think it weird or back-
ward that you're not using contraception. If you are blessed
with more children, you can expect similar reactions to your
growing family. The best response is usually not a scholarly
argument but simply to demonstrate the same peace and joy
you found so attractive when you first met Aggie's family.

JOSEPH, YOU AND Aggie inspire me with your faith and how
you live it. I think you exemplify the desire of St. Ignatius to
be Christians and not just to be *called* Christians. As I look
back to who you were three and a half years ago, your transformation reveals the freedom and new life Christ offers to
everyone in the Holy Spirit. Your continuing journey from
lust to greater chastity, from immaturity to man of God, has
not taken place in a day but has required years. You continue
to grow in faith and virtue. You manfully resist the habit of
pornography and lust and are now freer to form your son in
the life of Christ. Of course you still contend with temptations that are occasional rather than habitual. Keep watchful
and awake! The months following the birth of a child are
commonly an occasion of sexual temptation for men because
their wives are not as responsive to sex as they regain their
health and energy. Married women have shared with me that

they are tired from childbirth, nursing the newborn, and being mother to other children. A husband, they said, can become another person who wants something from her. Be mindful of Aggie's needs and care for her, as a man of God, showing your love and affection in ways that support her.

You are growing as a man of God as husband to Aggie and now as father to your son. Tomorrow, as you take Luke Francis in your arms and lift him onto the ark of the Church through the doorway of baptism, celebrate with joy your identity as a Catholic family. You are continuing the genealogy of Jesus Christ. Matthew's Gospel begins with the ancestry of Jesus: Abraham was the father of Isaac, the father of Jacob, on down a total of forty-two generations and eighteen centuries to Joseph, the husband of Mary. Now twenty-one centuries on this side of the Incarnation, a new genealogy has grown: those who are born into new life in Christ through the Holy Spirit at baptism. Jesus called Peter and Paul, and Paul called Timothy. St. John called St. Polycarp, and St. Polycarp called St. Irenaeus. Down through the centuries, men and women have told others about Jesus the Christ. Those called have been baptized and entered the family of the Church, brothers and sisters of Christ. Someone called our parents, and for most of us, our parents called us. Now you call your son to join the Kingdom, to live according to Christ's heart; to be a man of God.

Persisting in faith,

Fr. Terry

ABOUT THE AUTHOR

TERRENCE P. EHRMAN, C.S.C. is the assistant director for life science research and outreach at the Center for Theology, Science, and Human Flourishing at the University of Notre Dame. He investigates the relationship between theology and science, particularly the life sciences of ecology and evolution. His interests include understanding who God is as Creator, who we are as creatures, and what our relationship is to God, ourselves, and the natural world. Fr. Terry has a B.S. in biology from Notre Dame, M.S. in aquatic ecology from Virginia Tech, M.Div. from Notre Dame, and a Ph.D. in systematic theology from the Catholic University of America. He is originally from Baltimore, Maryland and was ordained a priest in 2000.